GW00738365

surfing
for friends

debbie brixey

foulsham
LONDON • NEW YORK • TORONTO • SYDNEY

foulsham

The Publishing House, Bennetts Close, Cippenham,
Slough, Berkshire, SL1 5AP, England

Foulsham books can be found in all good bookshops and direct from
www.foulsham.com

ISBN: 978-0-572-03447-4

Copyright © 2008 Debbie Brixey

Cover photograph © Superstock

A CIP record for this book is available from the British Library

Printed in Dubai

Contents

Introduction

Welcome to the whole new world of social networking online. It might seem like a contradiction to put online and social networking together, if you have no knowledge of the many ways the internet can help you stay in touch, meet new people, find groups with similar interests and learn new skills. A rather tall order, you might think, but with the internet all things are possible. Imagine having a combination of the world's largest library with the world's biggest encyclopaedia, mixed in with the hugest telephone directory you can think of, and that will give you some indication of the sheer scale of information available.

I know that when you hear about Messenger and networking – if you've heard of them at all – you tend to think of teenagers, and I will not deny that they do have a large part to play in the phenomenal growth of socialising sites on the web. But why should they have all the fun?

In this book I will give you the information you need to get online, even if you have never used a computer before. I will give you a guide to the web, and show you how to search for the things you want and to cut out the things you don't want. I'll explain the terms that you will come across and I will use language you'll understand; you won't need a jargon-buster just to get started.

I know that sometimes plucking up the courage to go out and meet new people can be daunting, so I aim to show you how to find out about groups and have some contact with them before you actually join. I'll advise you on how to find like-minded people, how to stay safe and how to use the internet to your own advantage in all sorts of ways.

Want to stay in touch with family and friends, wherever they are in the world? I will explain to you about the various ways of using e-mail and how you can use it even when you are away from your computer. I'll explain to you what the programs do, which ones are free and what you need to talk to that grandchild backpacking on the other side of the world.

How about finding old school friends or finally getting around to doing that family tree you promised yourself you would do? They are all just a click of a mouse away.

Always fancied trying your hand at something? Want to take up a hobby or maybe rekindle a love for an old pastime? I'll show you how to find the best sites. Remember: on the worldwide web, distance is no barrier.

Fancy a trip to the theatre but don't want to go on your own? I'll guide you to theatre groups in your area.

Retired but not yet ready to do nothing? How about volunteering? I'll show you how to contact groups that will put your valuable experience to good use. Fancy a part-time job? A list of jobs that suit your skills can be e-mailed to you, to save you trawling through papers.

If you are ready to explore the possibilities, then read on.

What is online socialising?

Online socialising is using the internet to connect to other people. In this book, 'connect' means so much more than it would normally do in computer terms. I am not just talking about telephone lines, broadband and cable, but the ability, should you so wish, to share thoughts and feelings with people anywhere in the world.

When I think about socialising I think of going out with friends, I think of popping to a pub, going out for a meal or the theatre. I also think of how far away people live from friends and family nowadays, and how difficult it is to keep in touch sometimes. Then I think about the internet, and how I can have a conversation with someone almost face to face at the other end of the country at midnight without actually leaving my chair.

What the internet has done is almost to redefine socialising. I am not suggesting that you don't go out or that actually seeing friends in person has lost its appeal, but why not do both?

It's not complicated or expensive

A few years ago it would have been a real luxury to have a broadband connection (don't worry: this is explained in the next chapter) in your home, but now it appears the majority of people are switching to faster connections.

As more and more people join the digital revolution, and silver surfers are one of the fastest growing groups to join, then the programs and equipment needed become both cheaper and easier to use. The early versions of home computers were not really equipped to cope with the things that are possible now. Today's systems make swapping documents and pictures with other users very easy and quick. We can record audible messages, chat in real time, see the person to whom we are speaking, retrieve and listen to music: virtually any sort of data can be put on to a computer and sent around the world in seconds. Even the most basic of today's computers has phenomenal power and can store masses of information.

I am not going to spend this book recommending that you buy things that you may only use once, or software that you need to be a computer genius to fathom. But what I will do is suggest what things are possible and why you might like them. The rest is up to you.

What can I gain from any of this?

Life changes as you get older, and you might find that you have more time on your hands now. Perhaps you have given up work, or your family has flown the nest. Whatever the reason, you might have no real idea of what you would like to do with your time.

This is where this book comes in. Use it to start new things, rekindle old things or even to remind yourself why you stopped doing whatever it was!

I hope you have a lot of fun, learn new things and, most of all, enjoy all that the internet has to offer.

Some words you might need

You don't need to be buried in jargon, but it does help to understand some basic computer terms before you start.

Apple Mac: Type of personal computer that works in a different way from a PC. Both systems do the same things, but may use slightly different programs.

Laptop: Portable computer, sometimes known as a notebook, that has screen, keyboard, processor and mouse all in one. It has all the same capabilities as a desktop computer.

Online: Connected to the internet.

Operating system: Software that allows you to use your computer. If you are using a PC, then it will usually be Windows, probably XP or Vista. If you are using an Apple Mac, then it will be OS, probably OS9 or OSX.

PC: Personal computer.

PDA: Personal Digital Assistant also known as palmtop – a very small computer that you can hold in your hand.

Web cam: A camera attached to your computer that can send live images from one computer to another.

Chapter 1

Getting Connected

For the purposes of this book, I am going to assume that you are new to the internet and that you have not yet have taken the plunge to go online. If you are already a seasoned surfer, you might just want to check out the security information on page 13 to reassure yourself that you are safely surfing, and then dive into the next chapter.

Don't worry about jargon

I'll explain any new words as I go along.

So it's a whole new world to you. What does it all mean? Put simply, the internet is a giant network of computers connected to one another via telephone lines. To look at the web or to send or receive e-mails, you must have an internet connection.

Connections

There are several ways to connect to the internet, but these are the three most widely used.

Dial-up

Dial-up connections use a modem (a piece of equipment normally inside your computer that translates between computer language and telephone language) and a telephone wire. This connects directly to the jack point that your telephone uses, and uses a special number supplied by your internet service provider (ISP) to access the web.

This is one of the slower means of connecting up, but is often the way people start on the internet. There are several packages available, such as pay-as-you-go where you only pay for the call time, or you could pay a fixed monthly fee that includes all your internet calls.

Broadband

Also known as ADSL, broadband is many times faster than a dial-up connection and has grown in popularity (and dropped in cost) over the last few years. According to Ofcom over 50% of adults have broadband in their homes. Many companies now offer a bundle that includes television, telephone and broadband, all within a single price.

One of the benefits of broadband is that you can talk on the telephone even while you are using the internet. To use broadband, you will need to have your telephone line enabled by your telephone company. You will also need to fit some filters on each of your telephone connection points and install an external modem. Most ISPs will supply them, although there may be a charge for this.

Cable

Cable internet access is usually provided by a company that runs a cable to a property with a view to providing TV and telephone services, as well as internet services, e.g. Sky. Cable internet access uses a box rather than a modem that is plugged into a PC.

Cable access is restricted to areas serviced by cable operators (often the more populated areas such as large towns and cities) and therefore may not be available for rural areas.

Browser

In order to connect to and use the internet, you will need a program called a browser, which will already be on your computer. Most people use Internet Explorer, but there are others around that do a similar job.

Protecting against viruses and spyware

There are two main things that hit the news and cause people to worry about the internet: viruses and spyware. However, don't let these put you off, because there is plenty you can do to ensure that you remain safe whilst online. Think of it as a little like putting on your seat belt when you get in a car; if you take sensible precautions, you should have a safe journey.

Viruses

A computer virus is a program that can copy itself and infect a computer without your permission or knowledge. Many personal computers are now connected to the internet and to home networks, which means viruses can spread to other computers by infecting files – they may also take advantage of services such as the web, e-mail and file sharing systems that enable several users to access the same data.

Some viruses are programmed to damage the computer by damaging programs, deleting files or reformatting the hard disk (which means wiping off all your information). Others do no actual damage, but replicate themselves and sometimes play text, video or audio messages. Although that sounds just irritating, it will also take up computer memory used by legitimate programs, which causes your computer to behave erratically and could result in system crashes (freezing or switching off) and loss of information.

To avoid infection (and prevention is definitely better than cure), your computer should have an anti-virus program installed. There are many programs available, and I would strongly recommend that you have one of them running before you start using the internet. Most importantly, you must keep it up-to-date, There are many viruses operating on the internet and new ones are discovered every day.

Anti-virus programs are available from leading software suppliers such as F-Secure, McAfee and Symantec. They can be bought from many high street retailers and online stores.

Downloading (transferring something from a website to your computer) a program over the internet direct from the manufacturer is quick and easy. Try these websites:

- **www.grisoft.com**
- **www.mcafee.co.uk**
- **www.microsoft.com/athome/security/downloads**
- **www.symantec.com/home_homeoffice/**
- **www.zonelabs.com**

Spyware

Spyware or adware is software that gathers information through an internet connection without the knowledge of the computer user, usually for advertising purposes. Spyware applications are typically hidden components of programs known as freeware or shareware that can be downloaded from the internet.

There are two main types of spyware. The least dangerous type is tracking software. Once installed, it monitors user activity on the internet and transmits that information in the background to someone else, usually in an effort to collect marketing data.

The second type is far more dangerous and is known as a key-logger. This is spyware that gathers information about e-mail addresses and even passwords and credit card numbers via online transactions. It works by capturing the keystrokes of a computer user and storing them. Most malicious key-loggers send this data to a remote third party.

Again, there are programs available to rid your computer and protect against these, which, if kept up-to-date should keep you safe. Look at the websites above and also try **www.downloads.co.uk**, which has links to sites offering all sorts of programs, including free anti-spyware programs.

Pop-ups

Next on our list for comfortable web browsing is blocking pop-ups. These are usually advertisements that open up in a new window in the middle of your screen when you are trying to do something. They do no harm but they are irritating and sometimes difficult to close – and you didn't ask for them, so you shouldn't have to put up with them!

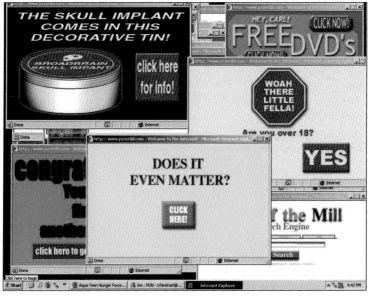

There are several answers to stopping these and they are all quite simple. The search engine Google, which we will discuss in greater detail in Chapter 4, has a built-in pop-up blocker in its toolbar, which is free to download. Internet Explorer 7, the browser that most people use, also has a built-in blocker that is easy to enable. You can also buy commercial pop-up blockers, some of which are included with anti-virus and anti-spyware programs (see page 14).

Firewalls

A firewall is a piece of software that stops other people having access to your computer while you are using it. Computers running Windows usually come with a personal firewall, which may also check what is being sent out to guard against spyware.

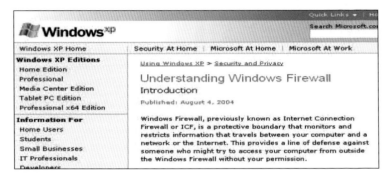

To check your firewall is on:

• Click on **Start**.

• Click on **Control panel**.

• Double-click on **Windows firewall**.

• Click on **On (recommended)**.

• Click **OK**.

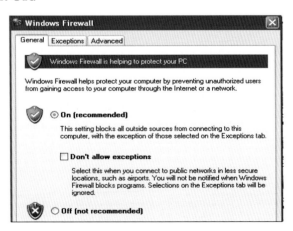

Are you sitting comfortably?

This is not a random question, but actually quite an important factor to do with your safe and continued computer usage. The importance of adopting a good ergonomic position cannot be stressed enough. There are several things you should consider before you start.

Firstly, make sure your chair is right for you:

- **Be comfortable:** The seat of your chair should not be too long for your legs, otherwise it will either catch you behind the knees or it will prevent you from leaning back fully. It should also be shaped to allow even weight distribution.

- **Adjust the height:** A general rule is to ensure that the front of your knees is level or slightly below level and your feet are firmly on the ground. Most people do not need a footrest.

- **Have a good back rest:** Your chair should have a back rest that can be adjusted up and down, forwards and backwards to best fit your shape. It should also be able to recline; movement of the back while seated helps to maintain a healthy spine.

- **Armrests:** If your chair has armrests, they should be broad, contoured, cushioned and comfortable. The more adjustable they are, the better. It can also be useful if they can be moved out of the way when not needed.

- **Check your desk:** Your desk height depends on your chair and your own measurements. The desk height can cause an exaggerated C-shaped spine, resulting in awkward posture that will give you back and shoulder pain.

- **Tilting seat:** This can be useful if you have any mobility problems that mean you find it hard to rise from your chair.

Sitting properly

Now I don't want to come over like your nanny, but if you want to enjoy your computer and not leave each session with a bad back, stiff neck or eye strain (or all of these things), follow these simple rules.

- Sit with your lower back supported against the backrest at the base of the chair.

- Tilt your chair seat forwards approximately 15 degrees, which induces a natural curve in your spine, and if necessary sit on a wedge-shaped cushion.

- Adjust the seat height and angle so that your hip joints are 10cm/4in higher than your knee joints.

- Adjust your work surface so that you keep your elbows at your side. Forearms parallel to the floor and supported by the desk. Relax your shoulders and keep your wrists in a neutral position.

- Place your keyboard flat on your desk surface.

- The top of the screen should be at eye level and facing you to avoid having to have your neck at an unnatural angle whilst working.

- Perform regular exercises to stretch the neck and shoulders.

- Check that the screen distance from the eyes: about 60cm/24in away is good.

- The screen brightness and contrast should be adjusted for the maximum viewing comfort. Good quality anti-glare screens help prevent squinting and eye strain.

- Try not to face a window or bright light source.

- Face into an open space beyond the computer screen.

- Clean the screen regularly because it attracts dust.

- Take a short break of around 10 to 15 minutes at least every two hours, to relax your eyes and body.

- Laptops are supposedly designed to work on your knee, but if you intend using yours for any length of time a desk is much better!

Screen

Apart from correcting your posture, there are a few other things you can do to make your time on the computer a pleasure rather than a pain.

Did you know that around two million people in the UK have a sight problem? This figure is estimated to rise to 2.5 million within the next 30 years. Many people need spectacles and often go for bifocal and varifocal glasses, but these can cause problems with a screen, resulting in nausea and a 'seasick' feeling. If this is you, try wearing reading glasses or single-focus glasses for the computer.

With most versions of Windows (and Mac), it is possible to make the icons and text larger on the screen. So, if you cannot easily see the screen, don't peer at it – change it!

Courtesy of Brian Basset and Microsoft Corporation

These instructions are for Windows XP, but will be very similar for other editions.

- Click on **Start**.

- Click on **Control panel** from the menu.

- Once the control panel has opened, double-click on **Display**.

- Click on **Appearance**.

At the bottom of this window, you will see a drop-down box (a box with an arrow denoting multiple choices) that says Font size above it and the word Normal. If you click on the arrow, you will be given a choice between normal, large or extra large. I recommend extra large, especially if you are working on a laptop with a smaller screen. As you can see from the illustration, the larger fonts apply to everything, including the icons on your desktop.

- Once you have adjusted the font size, click on **OK** until you are back to where you started.

If you continue to experience difficulties with the size of icons and text and your screen, you could try using a larger screen. Switching from a 15in to a 21in screen produces a 1½ times magnification without doing anything else!

Alternatively, use a magnifying program: Windows XP has one built in called Magnifier. This program allows a magnified area of the screen to be created that can move around with your cursor, keyboard or text editing movements.

• Click on **Start**.

• Click on **Programs**.

• Click on **Accessories**.

• Click on **Accessibility** and then **Windows Magnifier**.

• At the top of this window is a drop-down menu that allows you to select the degree of magnification you need. The magnified text will show at the top of the screen.

• Once you have adjusted the magnification, click on **OK** until you are back to where you started. To switch it off, click on **Exit**.

If Magnifier is not sufficient for your needs or you do not like the split-screen effect, there are a number of programs you can buy that will magnify the entire screen by as much as you need, e.g. Zoomtext available from **www.aisquared.com**.

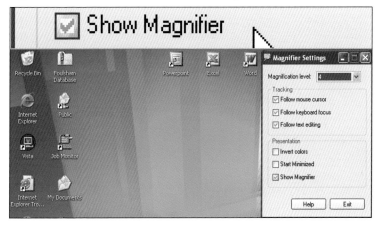

Dexterity

If you find it difficult to use a keyboard and mouse because of problems with your hands, there are a number of things you can do to help.

If you are having problems gripping, moving and clicking with a standard mouse, try a trackball mouse instead. This differs from a standard mouse in that you move the ball on top of the mouse rather than the mouse itself, so no gripping is needed.

If you are using a laptop and don't like using the mouse pad, buy a standard mouse and plug that in instead.

You can also change the way your computer responds to clicks and keyboard input.

- Click on **Start**.

- Click on **Control panel**.

- Double-click on **Folder options**, then choose **Single click to open**. Be aware that if you click on something to select it, it will open immediately.

So, if you are indeed sitting comfortably, and everything is set up, we will begin.

Chapter 2

E-mail

E-mail is an electronic way to send messages anywhere in the world. Not only can you send messages to anyone who has an e-mail address, but you can also send and receive things via e-mail such as photographs or documents.

Don't worry about an e-mail address

I'll explain how to go about getting an e-mail address, and the differences between various types.

So how do you send e-mail, what do you need and why would you want to?

Opening an e-mail account

Firstly, in order to send e-mail you must have an internet connection; most ISPs offer at least one (and sometimes up to five) e-mail addresses to go with your internet account. All e-mail addresses are unique. Think of them as a house number, road name and postcode; if you get any part of that wrong, someone else will receive your post, and e-mail is no different. E-mail providers also do a lot of 'return to sender' type messages, so you should take care when entering an e-mail address on an online form.

Some ISPs automatically assign you an e-mail address when you agree to use their service, and they will confirm this with you. Other ISPs give you a working address that is your telephone number @ their domain name (that is like their electronic company address). You would use this for accessing their service, and then set yourself up with an e-mail address that contains your name. These are often called sub-accounts.

Millions of people have e-mail accounts; many have several, preferring to separate their business and personal e-mails, and have private or very private e-mail addresses. Many business e-mail addresses use the company domain name, such as J.bloggs@flogit.com.

One of the important things to remember is that the internet works on a network, so when you send an e-mail you send it to your ISP who then sends it to your recipient's ISP who holds it in a 'mailbox' until the person who is expecting it checks their e-mail. So, although e-mail *can* be instant, if the person the other end doesn't check for new e-mail (and you'd be amazed how many people don't bother), then they won't get it.

There are two main types of e-mail accounts: firstly, what is known as a POP3 account (that's Post Office Protocol for those of you who like to know what the letters stand for). These accounts are normally on an individual user's computer, and they need to be accessed using a program such as Outlook or Outlook Express.

The other type of e-mail available is webmail. Again, you need an internet connection, but this time it can be accessed from any computer anywhere in the world. There are many advantages to this type of e-mail, one of which is that strictly speaking you don't actually have to own your own computer. You can access your own personal e-mail from a library, a friend or relative's computer or even an internet café. Such places charge by the hour for internet access, but they do tend to have up-to-date machines and faster broadband access, so it can be a good alternative.

Web-based e-mail does not suit everyone. You must sign in and remember your password each time you use it, especially if you are using a public computer where you cannot ask it to remember your details. Many web-based e-mail sites carry a lot of advertising and some people find this a little distracting. The format of these pages can be difficult to navigate because there is often a lot happening on the pages.

You might also at this point be asking why you would want an e-mail address if you don't know anyone else with one. Most websites will ask you for your e-mail address if you want to register with them or if you are asking them to send you details of their products or services. This would include networking sites, newsgroups and shopping sites. Often they use your e-mail address as a user name as it is unique to you. So even if you think you won't use it for e-mailing, it will be useful for other things.

Typing

One of the things that will convert e-mailing from a chore to a quick means of communication is the ability to type. You'll also find typing a boon when it comes to other forms of communication on the web. I recommend that if you cannot type now, you try to learn. Here are some sites that can help:

- www.popcap.com/gamepopup.php?theGame=typershark

- www.powertyping.com

- www.touch-typing-tutor.com/TypingTestTQ-FreeTypingTest.htm

I am not suggesting that you want a hugely fast touch-typing speed; but if you have to concentrate less on looking at the keyboard, you will have more chance to enjoy what is going on on the screen!

Using Outlook Express

Outlook Express is a Microsoft program that should come with your PC. (If you are using an Apple Mac, you will probably be using Mail.) One of the good things about Outlook Express is that it does not do anything other than deal with e-mail and therefore is remarkably straightforward. There are a number of other programs available that deal with POP mail, but this is the most common and most others behave in a similar way.

Firstly you need to find the program. Depending on how your computer has been set up, it might be on your desktop, or you should find it as follows:

• Click on **Start**.

• Click on **Programs**

The Outlook/Outlook Express program will be there. Look for the icon:

• Double-click on the icon to open the program

Don't worry about double-clicking

If you have trouble double-clicking on icons, try clicking once and then pressing enter on your keyboard.

When it has opened you should see a window that looks something like this:

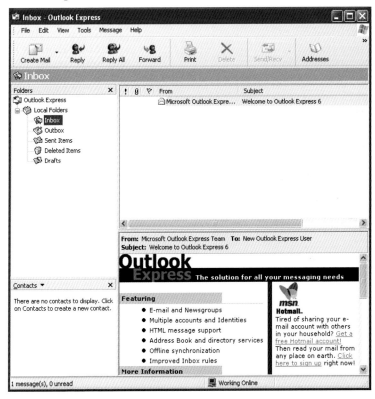

Your e-mail program usually consists of four main parts:

- The folder list where incoming, outgoing, sent and deleted items will be;

- The message pane where the contents of each folder will be displayed, normally set always to show your inbox when it first opens;

- The preview pane where the message you have highlighted will appear. so you can read it without having to double-click on it;

- The contacts list, which shows the names you have in your Address book.

Sending an e-mail

Firstly, you will need the e-mail address of the person you are sending it to. Remember all e-mail addresses are unique and must consist of the name of the person (or what they have decided to call themselves for the purpose of e-mail) the @ (at) symbol and the domain they are using. This is usually their ISP, e.g., yahoo.co.uk.

- Once you have opened Outlook Express, click on **Create mail**. This sometimes appears as **New** or in some programs as **Compose**. This will open a new window and take you automatically to the To: box where you need to type in the e-mail address of the person to whom you are writing.

Don't worry about your e-mail address

When you send an e-mail, your address automatically appears at the other end.

If you have added the address to your Contacts or Address book (see page 38), as you start typing in the To: box, Outlook Express should suggest the name of the person that you are e-mailing. Please note it will appear as you have entered it so if you have put Fred it will show Fred, not necessarily all of Fred's e-mail address!

Next you should either click or use your TAB key to get to the Subject: box. This is where you should type a word or two to say what the e-mail is about for instance 'Visit', 'Telephone Call' or 'Recipe'.

📖 To:	Fred|
📖 Cc:	
Subject:	Social networking

Once you have done this, either click or tab to the big white box below Subject. This is where you type your actual message and it can be as long or as short as you want – the box will expand as you type. Many people use this now instead of actually sending a letter. Imagine: no need to find an envelope, a stamp or go to the post box (especially when it is raining!).

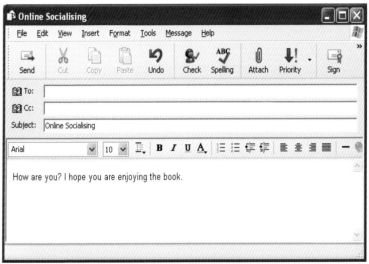

Once you have finished your message, all you have to do is click on **Send** and your e-mail will have gone to the Outbox. If you are on broadband the likelihood is it will have left the Outbox and be in the Sent Items folder before you have had a chance to blink.

If you are using a dial-up connection then, depending on how your computer was set up, you may have to click on **Send/receive** and it will reconnect to the internet for your message to go out.

You might be wondering: how do I know that it has gone? There are two things to look out for. Firstly, if it has left the Outbox and now appears in the Sent items folder, it has most certainly left your computer. You can check this by clicking on these folders in the list on the left of the screen. Secondly, you can usually presume an e-mail has gone if it does not come back to you. If you try to send an e-mail to an incorrect or non-existent address, the ISP at the other end will send you a message explaining that it could not be delivered.

Replying to an e-mail

If someone sends you an e-mail, it is very easy to reply. All you have to do is click on their message (this usually puts a blue line across the message called a highlight) and then click on **Reply** on the toolbar at the top of your window.

The good news with this is that it will automatically fill in the address of the person that you are sending it to (and as an added bonus on most machines will also add them to your Address book). It will also fill in the subject by putting Re: before whatever subject was originally on the message, which means that when you send it back the recipient will know that you are answering their e-mail.

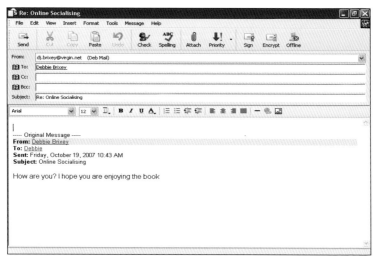

The cursor will automatically be in the message box ready for you to type your response. All you have to do is to type any message you wish them to have, click on **Send** and follow the same steps as when you send an e-mail from scratch.

You might notice on your e-mail program that there is both a Reply button and a Reply all button and the curious among you will be wondering what the difference is. Reply will send an e-mail only to the person who sent you the e-mail in the first place. Reply all will send an e-mail to the sender and any one else they sent the e-mail to. Put simply, if you receive an e-mail that is a sort of round robin affair, such as a joke or change of address, and you press reply all, every single person on that list will get your answer.

Forwarding an e-mail

Occasionally you might receive an e-mail that you think someone else would like, perhaps a joke, a bit of news or a photograph. It is easy to send this on to someone else with an e-mail address.

- Click on the message that you want to send on.

- Click on **Forward**. A new message window will open.

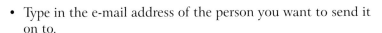

- Type in the e-mail address of the person you want to send it on to.

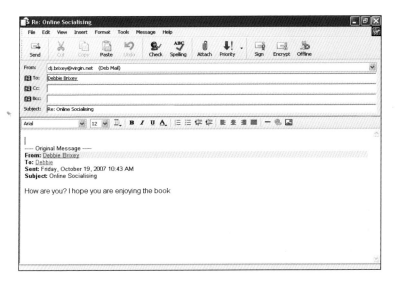

- The subject will say FW: to show that you are sending on something that you received previously. The original message and possibly attachment will already be in the message and you can either type in the message box to explain why you are sending it on, or if it is self-explanatory just send it.

- Click on **Send**.

Remember: you must be online to send and receive e-mails.

Spam

Just as you might receive junk mail through your letterbox, there is an e-mail equivalent known as spam. This is unsolicited bulk e-mail, normally sent for a commercial or fraudulent purpose (or at best just to annoy). You will often be able to tell that an e-mail is spam because it will be have silly names in it, or random strings of characters that don't make any sense. The subject line might be suspicious, perhaps offering you the chance to buy cheap Viagra, or notifying you that you have won a competition that you know you haven't entered.

The golden rule is: if in doubt, don't open it or reply to it. Simply delete it. Some ISPs will automatically filter out spam before it reaches your Inbox or have the facility for you to forward or report suspicious emails. The service varies, so check with your provider.

Phishing

Also look out for phishing. This is a particularly nasty type of spam where a fake e-mail is sent purporting to come from a legitimate source and asking you to confirm personal details. For example, you might receive an e-mail that looks as though it comes from your bank asking you to confirm your bank details and password. Normally there will be a link to a – false – website, which then captures the information to gain access to your bank account.

Many of these look genuine and even appear to have the logo of the bank on them, but remember: your bank would never send you an e-mail asking for that sort of information. Again, just delete it.

Opening attachments

When you look in your Inbox to see if you have any new e-mails, you might see one that has a paperclip symbol next to it. This means that it has an attachment, the e-mail equivalent of enclosing something with a letter.

Attachments can be anything; they can be a document like a letter, a photograph or they can even be a short film clip, complete with sound.

- Click on your e-mail and it will appear in the bottom half of your window in the Preview pane.

Don't worry **if you haven't a preview pane**

Just double-click on the message and then double-click on the attachment.

- Click on the paperclip to the right of the message. You should see the name of the attachment with an icon showing what type of file it is (for instance a square with a blue W on it means it is a word processing document) plus an instruction to Save the Attachment.

- If you click on the attachment, another window will open warning you of the potential for viruses, and asking if you are sure that you want to open it. If you know the sender and are happy that the contents are safe, click on **Open**.

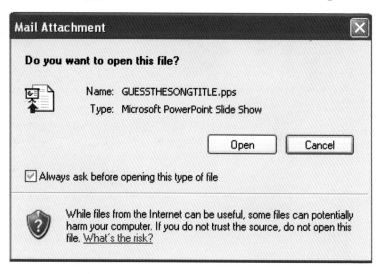

Your computer will automatically choose the right program to open the type of file.

Saving attachments

If someone sends you an attachment and you want to keep it but not necessarily the accompanying e-mail, you can save it on your computer.

- First click on the message to highlight it.

- Click on the paperclip, which will show you the attachment and give you an option to save it.

- Click on **Save attachments** and a new window will open that has an option at the bottom that says Save to. This allows you to tell the computer where you would like it filed. For example, if the attachment is a photograph or picture, then an obvious place is to store it is in the folder called My pictures.

- To find the folder click on **Browse**, which will show you a list of all the places available to store things.

- Find the My Documents folder. You should see a plus sign (+) next to it, which signifies that there are subfolders within. Click on **+** to see what is there.

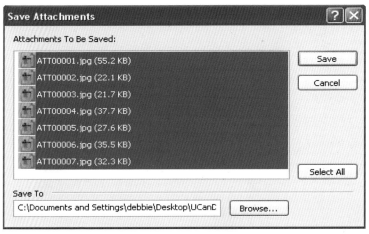

- The name of the folder you have chosen will appear in the Save to bar. If it is correct, click on **Save**. Otherwise, go back to Browse and try again.

- Find the folder in which you want to store the attachment, and click on **OK**.

You have now saved the attachment for as long as you want, and you can use it to send to someone else, to print it, include it in a document, set it as the background of your desktop or anything else you might want.

Sending an attachment

Now you have got to grips with the basics of sending and receiving e-mail, let's look at sending an attachment.

First open a new message window in exactly the same way as you would normally send an e-mail, and type in the e-mail address of where it is going. Move down to Subject and type in a subject, such as photos.

Now this is the bit where I can definitely share my experience. I always advise putting the attachment in now *before* you type the accompanying message. Why? Because it is easy to get so carried away with typing your message that you click on **Send** and forget to put the attachment with it. I have done it – and I think there are probably very few people who haven't had to send out a second e-mail that says, 'Whoops! Here's the attachment.'

- Click on **Attach**.

- A window will open showing the My documents folder and its contents. (It will open the last folder that was used.) If you are sending a photograph then it is likely that it will be in the My Pictures folder in My Documents.

- Find the item you are looking for by browsing through the folders, clicking on + if you need to get into a subfolder.

- Once you have found the item you want to send, click on it and then click on **Attach**.

File Edit View Tools Message Help
Reply   Reply All   Forward   Print   Delete   Previous   Next   Addresses

From: Debbie Brixey
Date: 19 October 2007 12:25
To: Debbie
Subject: Fw: Polar bear playing with a sled dog
Attach: ATT00007.jpg (32.3 KB)

Your message will now consist of To: CC, Subject and Attach. In the Attach box there will be the name of the file that you intend sending. If you want to send more than one file, repeat the steps above as many times as required.

Size of attachments

A word of warning on sending attachments. Some files are quite large, especially photographs if they have been taken in a high resolution. There are two things that you need to bear in mind when sending these.

The first is whether the recipient is on a dial-up or broadband connection. If it is dial-up, a large file could take literally hours to come across, tying up the phone line and running up their bill! The second thing is that some ISPs, particularly web-mail providers, have a maximum limit for outgoing and incoming attachments that is often in the region of 10mb. This might sound a lot, but I have seen many photographs being sent in the region of 1.5mb each.

Remember also that not everyone has the same programs on their computer, so occasionally you and your recipient may not be able to open certain attachments. Check before you send.

Your Address book

The Address book is also known as Contacts and is the place to store all those e-mail addresses that you acquire as soon as everyone knows you have an internet connection.

Earlier, you learned that an e-mail address can be added to your Address book automatically, but what happens if you are sending to a new contact? Then you need to add it to your Address book manually.

- In Outlook Express, click on **Addresses**. A window opens showing you the names and addresses of the people you already have stored.

- To add to this list, click on **New**.

- Select **New contact** from the list that appears.

- In the first and last name boxes type in the name of the person as you would identify them. Remember: this is for you to identify them so if, for instance, you always call someone 'Big Bill' because you know several Bills and don't necessarily refer to their surnames then that would be fine.

- Next click into **E-mail address** and type in the e-mail address that person uses. Make sure that it is exactly the way you were given it including any dots, underscores or numbers or it won't be delivered.

- Next click on **Add** and the e-mail address will appear in the box below with the word Default after it.

- Click on **OK** and you will be back to your list of contacts.

Don't worry **about defaults**

In computer talk, a default is simply an option used in preference to other choices. If you have more than one e-mail address for the same person – perhaps one at home and one at work – the default address is the preferred one.

You can carry on adding addresses and when you have finished just click on the **X** in the top right-hand corner to return to your e-mail program.

You may notice looking at the New address window that there are several tabs across the top including 'home', 'business' and 'personal'. This allows you to add more details about your contact, such as their postal address (or snail mail as it is often called) and any telephone numbers you have for them. Some people use this information to produce labels, say, for Christmas cards.

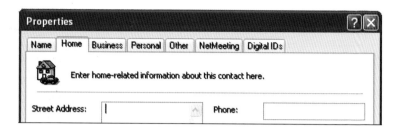

Creating contact groups

Sometimes you might want to send the same e-mail to several people at the same time on a regular basis, e.g., if you have to send out minutes to a club that you belong to. Rather than go through the lengthy business of adding each member to an e-mail every time you need to send it, you can create a group that will send to all the people in one go.

- In Outlook Express, click on **Addresses**.

- When the new window opens, click on **New**.

- Select **New group**.

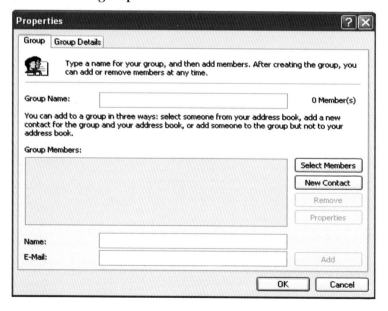

- Give the group a name e.g., Reading Group or Bungee Jumpers – whatever is appropriate.

- Next, click on **Select members**. This will open up your Address book and show all your contacts.

- Then all you need to do is click on the person you want to include, and click on **Select**. Their name will appear in the right-hand window. This does not mean that you won't be able to send them e-mails individually in the future; they will still appear as themselves in your Address book.

- When you have finished selecting, click on **OK**, and all the group members' names will be showing in the window.

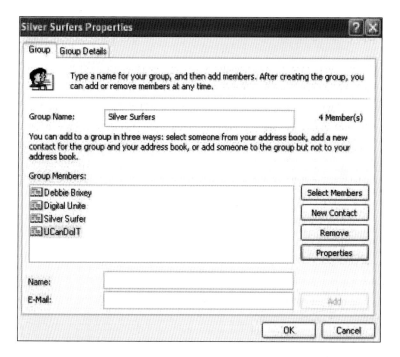

If you want to add someone to the group who is not already in your Address book, you can do this using the New contact button as above. If the group changes and people join or leave, you can also change the addresses that appear in here. When you have finished click on **OK** again.

- To send an e-mail to the entire group, click on **Addresses**.

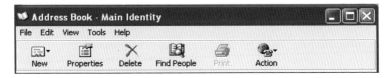

- Click on the name of the group and click on **Action**.

- Click on **Send mail**. Everybody in the group will be sent an e-mail, whether the group is three people or 30.

The best way to get to grips with e-mail is to practise, so send yourself a few e-mails to get the hang of it!

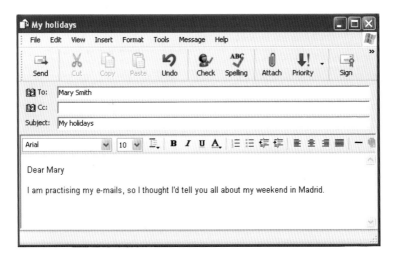

Chapter 3
Talking Via Your Computer

There are many ways to communicate using your computer, and until fairly recently e-mail was one of the quickest and easiest. However, with so many people now on broadband there has been a huge increase in other ways, and this chapter is designed to explain what they are, how you can use them and to give a comparison between the various options.

One of the most popular options is Messenger. There are several variations of Messenger, the most popular of which are Windows and MSN. They are often known as instant messaging (IM) sites, and have an entire language and method of their own. Many of the sites are particularly popular with teenagers who seem to communicate only via this means or texting on their mobiles! If you have grandchildren or younger nieces and nephews, you will probably find this is a guaranteed way of holding their attention, if only for a few minutes.

There are two main ways that Messenger works: by typing a message or by talking directly to a person via the computer. If you are typing (especially with a teenager) I would suggest brushing up on textspeak. This is a system of abbreviations and contractions that means you type your message using fewer characters. For example 'how r u?' might earn you some kudos with the youngsters. The idea is that more than one person can take part in a text 'conversation', and you can have several conversations going on at once with different people who may also be having several conversations – the combinations are endless. See also page 59.

Examples of textspeak

AFK: Away from keyboard.

BBFN: Bye-bye for now.

BFN: Bye for now.

CMIIW: Correct me if I'm wrong.

CU: See you.

FITB: Fill in the blank.

G2G: I've got to go.

IMHO: In my humble/honest opinion.

L8R: Later.

LOL: I'm laughing out loud.

TTFN: Ta-ta for now.

You are probably thinking: but I thought this was e-mail and I typed a message and sent it – what is the difference? The keyword is *instant*; in other words, it happens in real time. You type your message into a box, click on **Send** and it appears on the other person's computer. The only thing stopping it being any faster is the speed people type.

Getting started with Messenger

There are many versions of IM programs, and some are used more than others. Before you sign up for one, check if anyone you want to talk to has an IM account and what program they are using. Figures differ, but the most popular programs are often quoted as having at least 30 million users. I am going to concentrate on Windows Messenger, as it is very popular and many of the other programs are very similar in appearance and behaviour.

Firstly, in order to use an IM service you need to have an account. By this I mean that you have to sign up to the service, which is usually free. You will also need an e-mail address.

If you have a computer with Windows XP, you will probably find that you already have a version of Messenger on your machine. In fact, you may find that it has been set to open when you start the computer, even though you haven't as yet created an account. Look at the bottom right-hand corner of your screen (called the notification area) and check for the head and shoulders of a little green man.

If you don't already have Messenger then you will need to create an account, and download the Messenger program. If you have a Hotmail e-mail account, then you can use that to go straight to download Messenger, and to sign in.

How to get a Hotmail account

- First, open your internet browser (probably Internet Explorer).

- Type in the address bar www.hotmail.com.

- When this window has opened click on **Sign up**.

Don't worry **if the text looks too small**

If you can't read text in Internet Explorer, go to the View menu, click on **Text size** and increase the font size to **Large** or **Largest**.

A page entitled Windows Live will open. This is a fairly recent development that combines various parts of the MSN service as one package, allowing you to access e-mail, web space (don't worry about this for now) and instant messaging all together.

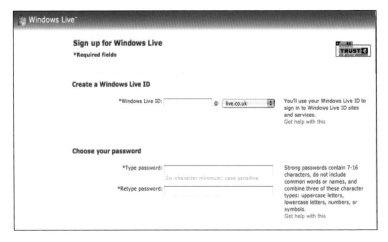

- Under Windows Live Hotmail, click on **Sign up**. The screen Create a Windows Live ID will open.

- In the box Windows Live ID, type in the name by which you would like to be known during IM conversations. As with any e-mail address, where possible try to keep it simple so that you can remember it and people can identify you by it.

- Next click on **Check availability**. This will tell you whether you can have what you asked for. Unfortunately, there are a lot of people with e-mail addresses, so you may have to try a few times before you get one you can use. Try adding full stops, underscores or numbers to the address to make it individual, but something you will easily remember.

- Now type in the password you would like to use for this account. The password box here tells you what level of security your chosen password will give you against hackers and similar. If you are happy with your choice, repeat it in the second box. If not, try another one.

Don't worry **if you can't read your password**

When you type in your password it will appear as dots or stars. This is known as encryption and is to stop people getting access to your Messenger details.

- Type in your personal details – name, address, gender, date of birth – in the boxes provided. You will then be asked for your name, year of birth and so on, so that if the need arises you can be identified and all being well no one can misrepresent you.

- You will also be required to fill in an alternative e-mail address and set up a security question so that if you forget your Hotmail details you can be sent them.

- At the bottom of the page you will find a rather strange box with several jumbled up letters and sometimes numbers. Type in whatever is in the box. This is to prove you are a human and to stop automated programs creating accounts so they can send out more spam.

Type the characters you see in this picture

Picture: 5J8DBX B8   This helps us prevent automated programs from creating accounts and sending spam.
8 characters   Get help with this

*Type characters: 5J8DBXB8

Review and accept the agreements

Clicking **I accept** means that you agree to the Windows Live Service Agreement and Privacy Statement.

[I accept]   [Cancel]

- Read the details of the service agreement and then click on **I accept**.

This will then take you to a window that allows you to choose how you would like your e-mail account to appear. The Classic version is quite simple and probably better suited to internet beginners, as it has fewer things happening on it. The newer version is designed for a large screen, but has the advantage of allowing the user to see a preview of the message in the same place as the inbox. All this becomes clear once you start to use it.

Passwords

There are two schools of thought when it comes to choosing a password. If you use the exact same password for everything (banking, e-mail, membership, shopping) then should someone get hold of it or be able to guess, they will have access to far more things than you would want. However, if you have too many passwords you will never remember them.

Here are a few password tips:

• A combination of letters and numbers will make your password harder to guess.

• Some passwords are case sensitive.

• Don't use anything too obvious, such as your name!

• Use at least seven characters

You will find more information at **www.getsafeonline.org**.

Using Messenger

Now for the fun bit, actually using Messenger. Once you have downloaded Messenger, you should see this icon on your desktop.

• Double-click on the icon and a Sign in window will appear.

Have an **MSN Hotmail**, **MSN Messenger**, or **Passport** account? It's your **Windows Live ID**.

Sign in

Windows Live ID: the_silver@hotmail.co.uk
(example555@hotmail.com)

Password:

- Fill this in with your Hotmail address and then click on **Sign in**.

Don't worry **about automatic login**

It is possible to set Messenger to sign in automatically as soon as the computer is switched on, which means that people know you are online straight away. However, you may not always want people to know you are there – for instance, if you just popped on to send a quick e-mail and then were going out.

Don't worry **if you don't have an icon**

Simply click on **Start**, **Programs**, then **Windows Messenger** to open the program.

The first window you will see will look something like this and will want you to add contacts. After all, there is very little point in setting all of this up if you are not going to talk to people!

On the right-hand side of the window you will see the Messenger icon with a plus sign. This is the **Add contact** button: click on this to open the following screen:

Having asked all your friends and family for the e-mail addresses or user names for Messenger, you can now type them in.

- In the first box, enter the e-mail address of your contact.

- Moving down, click in the message box and type a quick message such as 'Hi I am now on Messenger please add me to your contacts.'

- If you wish, tick the box below to send the same message via e-mail, just in case your friend doesn't log on to Messenger very often.

Don't worry about retyping

You don't need to type the same message again and again. Highlight the message, then press **CTRL + C** and this will copy it. On your next contact, click in the box and press **CTRL + V** and it will fill it in.

- Click in the **Nickname** box and type in whatever name you use to identify this contact.

- If you want to add them to a group such as friends or family, then use the drop-down menu to select the relevant one.

- When you have finished, click on **Add contact**.

- You need to do this for each person you want to include on your list of Messenger contacts. Most IM services will work in much the same way.

IM status

So the next question you might want to ask is, how do I know when they are online, i.e., available to receive an IM?

Look at these two screens: the left-hand one shows my one contact under friends and shows that 0 out of 1 people is available. However, if you look at the box on the right you will see the icon has turned green and is now showing 1 out of 1 person is available. My friend Deb in now online and able to receive an IM.

You can choose how people perceive your status at the other end of the conversation. At the top of the screen, by your name, there is a drop-down menu of options:

If, for instance, your telephone rang and you had to answer it, you could set your status to **Busy**. Or if you are waiting for a specific contact to come online at a prearranged time, but in the meantime you don't want to receive any other IMs, you can set your status to **Appear offline**. Remember, though, that if *you* can do it, so can other people!

If you click on **Personal settings**, you can adjust how your details appear.

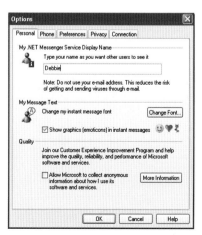

A nudge and a wink

If you can see someone is online, and you send them a typed message and get no response, you can get their attention by either sending a 'nudge', which makes the Messenger screen shake up and down as if it were being rattled, or a 'wink'. This is provided free as part of Messenger.

- Click on the **Nudge** icon (far right).

- To wink at someone, click on the **Wink** icon (the middle one. A new window will open giving you a choice of winks – I rather like the hand. When played it looks and sounds as though the hand is tapping on your monitor from the inside.

- If you want to know what any of them do, click on **Preview** and you can find out!

You can download extra winks by clicking on **See more offerings** in the corner of the Winks screen.

The other icon, the smiley face, is for sending an emoticon, i.e., a symbol to signify the mood or tone that your message is sent in. You may find from time to time that you get e-mails or text messages containing strange symbols such as :), which signifies a smile, or even :-! 'foot in mouth – oops', which re-create emoticons using regular keyboard strokes.

Personalising your Messenger

If you are going to use Messenger on a regular basis, then you might like to make it more your own by changing the background and the profile picture that people see.

- Click on **Tools** on the menu bar and select **Backgrounds**. A selection of about 10 choices will appear.

- Click on whichever one you like (I rather like the one with the clock), then click on **Set default**. This will now be the background everyone sees when you are communicating with them.

Next, what about your profile picture?

- Click on **Tools** then click on **Change display picture** and here you have a choice of using one of the pictures that they supply automatically.

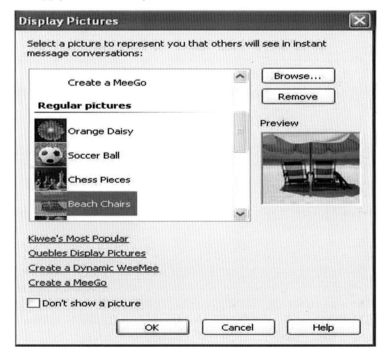

- Select the picture you want, then click on **OK**.

You can also use one of our own pictures, perhaps one of you and your dog or some other favourite snap.

- Click on **Browse**, then find your picture stored on your computer (see page 35). Select this then click on **OK**. If you get bored with the picture or the dog complains, then you can remove it and replace it with something else any time you want.

One of the other useful features of instant messaging is the ability to share files whilst talking. I have sent and received many photographs while having a conversation with people, and it is a great way to share things and very simple.

- On the **Actions menu**, click on **Send other**, and then click on **Send a single file**.

- Select the contact you want to send the file to, and then click on **OK**.

- Browse through your documents to select the file you want to send, and then click on **Open**.

If someone you are talking to sends you a photograph or other file, it will appear in your window with a message asking whether you want to accept or decline it. If you know who and what it is, click on Accept. The file will be downloaded to your computer, usually to a folder called My received files.

Contacting someone with Messenger

There are two other ways to communicate using an IM service.

The first way is to 'call' a contact's computer. To do this you must have a microphone attached to your computer. Many people like to have a microphone and headset so they can keep the conversation private, but a separate microphone and the speakers on the computer will do just as well. If your microphone is set up on the computer, you need to check that Messenger knows it is there, and that it is set up in the best way.

- Click on **Tools**, then **Audio and visual set-up**.

- Follow the on-screen instructions (known as the wizard) to set up your system.

By making a call to a contact's computer, you are using your computer a little like a telephone but without the bills. The computer at their end will ring (assuming of course that they have their volume or speakers switched on), and they then answer the call.

The other way, and possibly one of the most exciting advantages of this system, is video. For this, you must have a web cam. For the person at the other end to see you, there has to be a camera plugged into your computer. For you to see them, they must have a web cam on their computer. If you both have web cams you can have a conversation with sound and live video almost as if you were in the same room, no matter where in the world either of you are. The images sent by a web cab will simply appear on the recipient's computer screen.

Imagine if you have grandchildren living miles away, and you don't get to see them quite as often as you might like. If they and you each have a web cam you can talk to them and see how they have grown whenever you want.

However, if you want to reach a wider audience (like the world) there are websites where you can broadcast your video to the whole world. See page 95.

Buying a web cam

A web cam is a small, real-time video camera, often with a built-in microphone, that plugs into a computer. Real-time means it broadcasts a live or virtually live image across the web. (There might be a small time lag.) Many websites incorporate a web cam to show a relevant scene. For example a television nature programme might have a web cam inside a bird box. One of my favourites is a 'street cam' showing Times Square in New York (**www.earthcam.com/usa/newyork/timessquare**).

The second use for a web cam is for you to use it on your computer to talk almost face-to-face to people. Over the last few years the cost of web cams has dropped immensely, and you can now buy a good web cam for a relatively low price. However, with the cheaper cameras you will probably need to buy a separate microphone and/or headset.

The other key thing to look at when buying a web cam is the definition of the image, i.e., the number of pixels it captures. The higher the pixels the clearer the image and ideally you should have a resolution of 640 × 480 DPI.

Other features include face tracking, where the camera automatically follows a central point on the person's face, so they stay in focus (although this always make me feel slightly nauseous!). Some cameras also offer Digital Zoom. This is not the same as you would find on a stills camera; it just increases the area rather than actually zooming in.

Don't worry **about getting too technical**

Any basic web cam with adequate resolution will do to get you started. However, if you intend using your camera for things other than instant messaging, then it would be worthwhile asking whether it has the capability of taking reasonable still images, functioning as a lower resolution digital camera, and also what software the camera comes with if, for instance, you want to record a video to e-mail to someone, or to record on to a disk to send (rather than using it as an IM). If this is the case then I would recommend that you shop around and spend a little more money on your camera.

One of the best places to compare prices and reviews for products is the internet. I always find Amazon (**www.amazon. co.uk**) very useful, as the customer reviews often tell you a little more (and often more directly) about the actual working realities of a bit of equipment or its accompanying software.

A word about Skype

One of the other big breakthroughs on the internet is something called Voice Over Internet Protocols (VOIP). This means that you can utilise an internet connection as a telephone, either to call another computer (very like we looked at in Messenger), or to use the computer to call a telephone.

One of the most popular programs for this is Skype, which is free to download from **www.skype.com**. Skype does all the things that Messenger does as far as IMs, voice and video calls, but it also allows users to have conference calls (several people joining in a voice conversation at the same time), something that telephone providers normally charge for. This means that if, for example, you had two brothers and a sister based in Australia, Canada and the UK respectively and they all had a Skype account, you could have a three-way conversation.

Once you have downloaded Skype, you need to create an account just like you did with Messenger but without having to create a new e-mail address.

Once you have created your account you will need to add contacts, and this is the fun bit, as Skype will look in your e-mail Address book for you and tell you who already has a Skype account; but be warned sometimes it gets it wrong and you could make new friends!

Skype looks at a variety of e-mail accounts and if you have friends who do not have a Skype account, it will offer you the opportunity to invite them to sign up for an account – all quite easy really.

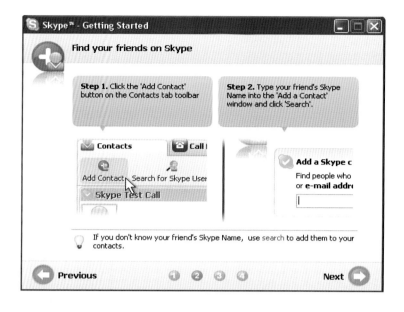

Once you have added the contacts, a message goes out to them asking whether they will add you to their contacts list.

As with all the IM services, you have the option of appearing online or away, busy, etc.

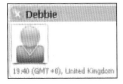 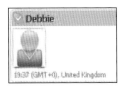 

Skype also offers users the option to buy credits, a little like a virtual phone card, that enables them to use their broadband connection to call a landline. This often works out as a cheaper option when calling abroad (but do check rates first). Some IM services also offer this.

Here's how it looks when you open a conversation.

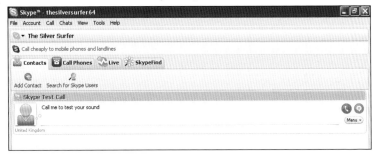

You can also personalise your Skype profile.

Using your computer to talk to people has several advantages (other than the obvious cost-saving implications), as the ability to swap files, links to web pages and photographs almost instantaneously certainly beats having to remember to post whatever you promised to send.

Chapter 4

Finding Information on the Web

In this chapter we are going to look at how to find things you want on the World Wide Web, and for this you need to use a search engine.

A search engine looks through millions of pages on the web by using software known as 'spiders' to 'crawl' through the web. Needless to say, there are lots of search engines available, and many of them will give you the same results. Everyone has their own personal preference, but for now we will look at the most popular and describe how they work, what you should and should not ask and, most importantly, how to narrow down your searches to get the answer you need rather than a huge list.

One of the most popular search engines available is Google, so I will use that as an example. Most others work in the same way. (Figures show that more than half of recorded searches on the internet are done using Google, followed by Yahoo.)

How to perform a search

As an example, this is how to use Google to find a holiday. Firstly, you need to go to the Google website.

- First, open your internet browser (Internet Explorer).

- Type in the address bar www.google.co.uk (if you are in the UK).

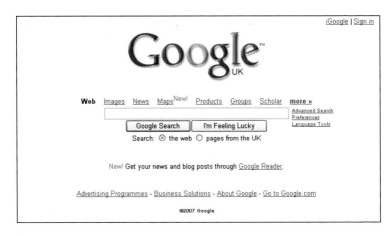

You will see that there is a box for you to type in. You will also see similar boxes on other websites, but these are usually to search the content of the site rather than the whole web.

• Click in the box and type Holiday and then either press enter on your keyboard or click on **Google search**.

Don't worry **about other search options**

If you click on **I'm feeling lucky**, this will bring up the result that is most likely to meet your search criteria. You can also choose to search the whole web or, to narrow your ranges of results, just pages from the UK.

Look at the blue bar, and you will see this search brought you a staggering 343,000,000 results, so we need to be a bit more precise. Let's pick a country. I am going to go for France, but feel free to try any country you fancy (even if you are never going to go there!).

- Click in the box after the word holiday, and type France after the space, click on **Search** or press **Enter** on your keyboard.

This time the results are less, but still a rather hefty 59,500,000.

So now for the clever bit, where we can start to whittle down the results into information we actually want. Refine your search still further by picking which part of France you are interested in, for example the Loire Valley.

- Click into the box after the word holiday, type Loire Valley, then click on **Search** or press **Enter** on your keyboard.

Once again, this has brought the figures down to something a little more manageable with 716,000.

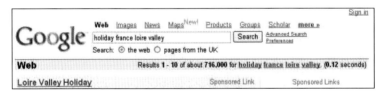

Now I don't know about you, but I have always fancied staying somewhere a little bit different, so let's be even more precise and add the type of accommodation as well this time. However, I also want to add a further instruction.

- Click in the box after the last word and type +Gite without a space, then click on **Search**.

This has brought it down to 84,600, which is a great difference from our original figure. By adding a plus sign with no gap we have told the search engine that we are only interested in results that include the word that follows the plus sign. You can also exclude words by putting a minus sign in front of a word. For instance –camping would bring it down to 74,100.

Searches are conducted in the order that the words are put into the search box so a search 'France Holiday Loire valley' gives us 539,000 rather than our original 716,000. Experiment with the word order in your searches for a better sense of how it works.

Search engines also use keywords to link to pages. These describe what the web page is about, but they may not always be under what you might expect. For instance, if you are looking for a computer company and can't find it, then try PC or IT instead. Similarly, if you are looking for something in a specific geographical area, try searching using the postcode, rather than the general location or borough.

Favourites

If you find a website that you like and you think you will want to visit again, you can save it to a folder called Favourites (also known as bookmarking).

To do this, you should be on the homepage of the site (the first page it opens) and then, depending on which version of Internet Explorer you are using, click on either the yellow star with the word **Favourites** in IE6, or on the yellow star with a plus sign on it in IE7. If you want to rename the site to something easy to remember, type it in and then press **OK**. The site will be there now for as long as you want it.

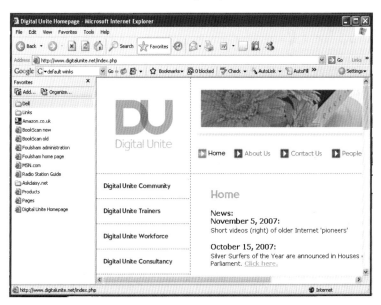

Making Google your default search engine

If you are using Internet Explorer 7 as your web browser, you may notice that there is a search box in the top right-hand corner of your window. If this is not already set to use Google you can change it do so, thus alleviating the need actually to go to the Google homepage.

- Click on the down arrow to the right of the search box to open a drop-down menu.

- Click on **Change search defaults**. A new window will open with a list of available search engines.

- If Google is there, click on it, then click on **Set as default** and **OK**.

- If Google does not appear in this list, click on **Cancel** and return to the drop-down menu.

- Click on **Find more providers** at the bottom of the window. A web page with a list of search engines will open. Click on **Google** in the list.

- Click in the box next to the option to make this your default, then click on **Add provider**. Close the window with the list of search engines, by clicking on **X** in the top right-hand corner as normal and you should be back to where you started, but with Google appearing in the search box.

If you are using an older version of Internet Explorer, I recommend that you download the Google toolbar to save you the trouble of having to navigate away from the page you are on to perform a new search. To do this, simply go to the Google homepage and click on **Download Google toolbar**.

Don't worry if it says Google in the search box

When you start typing your query, it will disappear.

Don't worry **about http**

If there is no www in the address of a website, you will need to type http:// in front of it. Otherwise, you can ignore it.

Here are some alternative search engines for you to try:

- http://search.aol.co.uk

- http://search.netscape.com

- http://uk.altavista.com

- http://uk.yahoo.com

- www.ask.co.uk

- www.excite.co.uk

- www.live.com

- www.lycos.co.uk

- www.mirago.co.uk

Sponsored links

Something else to bear in mind when using a search engine is the use of sponsored links, like those you will see on the right-hand column of the Google site. These are advertisers that have paid to have their link featured under a relevant keyword and to appear more prominently on the page – for instance, at the top with a coloured background. Some sites have paid-for listings only and therefore may not have an entry from the exact company you are looking for, if that company has chosen not to advertise with that search engine.

Chapter 5

Internet Groups

What is a newsgroup?

The first thing I should explain is that newsgroups do not necessarily deal with news! What they actually consist of is a huge array of bulletin boards where people can have online discussions on a wide variety of subjects. There are tens of thousands of newsgroups, and they continue to grow in number.

Users subscribe to a newsgroup in order to 'post' a message or reply to someone else's comments. You can share information, ask questions or just meet people with similar interests. Newsgroups can be accessed either on the web, via your e-mail or by using a program called a newsreader that does more complicated searches and has to be installed. Most people use either their internet browser or an e-mail program such as Outlook Express to access newsgroups.

An important thing to remember is that many newsgroups are not moderated (monitored by an individual or individuals to ensure that the subject matter is correct for the group) and therefore posts can be offensive to some, so look carefully at groups that interest you.

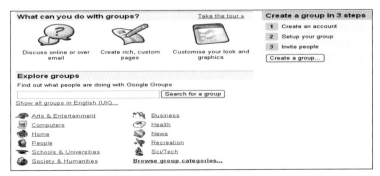

How to find a group

Using your newfound skills from the previous chapter, you could search for a group. There are a number of sites that are known for their groups, and I have listed a few of them here, but a search on a topic will no doubt show even more:

- http://groups.ebay.co.uk/index.jspa

- http://groups.google.co.uk

- http://uk.groups.yahoo.com

For instance, eBay groups cover a wide range of topics, but may be of interest in particular if your hobby is collecting, e.g., the ceramics and glass section has almost 30 different groups divided into subcategories such as Toby jugs, Poole pottery and Georgian glass.

Google and Yahoo groups are even wider ranging, and can cover most topics. The screen below gives some idea of what is available. As you can see, not only can you choose a topic, but you can also choose a language to read and respond in.

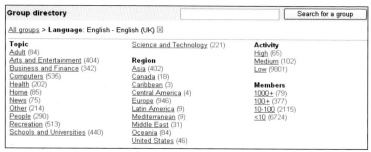

Google groups allow you to see whether groups are high or low activity (whether a lot of people are reading and responding, or whether nobody really bothers). They also show how many members a group has, to give you an idea of how popular the subject or group is. Some groups have a lot of members, but only a few contributors. Many other subscribers tend to lurk reading the messages but not often contributing. You don't have to contribute, but if you can help or inform, then go ahead!

Sometimes it can be a little difficult to fathom out quite what category a group you might be interested in will appear in, so I would suggest using the Search groups facility. For example, if you are interested in researching your family history (or even someone else's if you are feeling kind), I would suggest typing in Genealogy.

Groups **1-15 of 471**.

soc.**genealogy**.britain - Show matching messages from this group
Genealogy in Great Britain and the islands.
Category: People > Genealogy, Language: English
High activity, 967 subscribers, Usenet

alt.talk.royalty - Show matching messages from this group
Discussion of royalty and nobility.
Category: Society > Issues, Language: English
High activity, 613 subscribers, Usenet

soc.**genealogy**.medieval - Show matching messages from this group
Genealogy in the period from roughly AD500 to AD1600.
Category: People > Genealogy, Language: English
High activity, 501 subscribers, Usenet

news.groups - Show matching messages from this group
Discussions and lists of newsgroups.
Category: News, Language: English
Medium activity, 775 subscribers, Usenet

As you can see. there are a large number of groups dealing with genealogy, which has become a very popular subject. Some groups only deal with things such as software for creating family history records, some deal with particular countries and some with particular timescales. These group listings will tell you what their principal areas of interest are, how many subscribers they have and the level of activity.

Groups are also identified by hierarchies, a description of what they are about. For instance:

- **Comp:** computer groups that would discuss software, hardware and operating systems. These are often really helpful groups where you can post a question (about something that you are having problems with, for instance) and get an answer (or answers) from people who have had the same problems.

- **Humanities:** mainly art and literature.

- **Misc:** could be anything that cannot be put into one of the other categories.

- **News:** usually a group set up to discuss the groups themselves.

- **Rec:** recreation to discuss hobbies, games, music, sports and similar.

- **Sci:** science groups that discuss research, technology and inventions.

- **Soc:** society groups that discuss social and cultural issues.

- **Talk:** current events, news and debates on any subject.

These are the main headings and are usually moderated groups. If you come across a group starting with alt., this stands for alternative and may not be to everyone's taste.

There are a vast number of other hierarchies on the web. For instance uk.adverts.*something* would be, as the name implies, a UK-based group selling 'something', e.g., computers or computer parts.

You can also simply search and see what comes up.

Explore groups

Find out what people are doing with Google Groups

[   ] (Search for a group)

Show all groups in English (UK)...

Support groups

There are a number of groups on the internet that are both newsgroups and forums, set up to help people of all ages with specific events or issues in their lives. They are often run either by volunteers or people who have been through the same things, or by government agencies or charities. Their aim is to offer advice, information and a place to discuss things that affect their members' daily lives.

A large number of the support groups deal with health issues and, although not necessarily aimed at the over 50s, will contain a mixture of ages, all with a common goal. Many of the support groups can also offer advice on whether there are local groups near to you, so that you can also have the option of talking to people face to face.

Use a search engine to find whether there is a support group for you or near you. If for instance you are looking for a support group dealing with diabetes in Cardiff, then type this into Google or other search engine and you should find your nearest group. Remember: sometimes a postcode will work better than a town or city name.

To take some examples: if you have been recently widowed you may find **www.nawidows.org.uk** a helpful resource both for legal and practical advice, and for support. Anyone suffering from arthritis could try **www.arthritiscare.org.uk/Get Involved/Discussionforum** or for diabetes try **www.support. diabetes-insight.info**. The important message behind all of the support groups, whatever they cover, is that you are not alone.

Having found an interesting group, you will need to subscribe to post any replies. Some groups will allow you to read their postings without subscribing, but private or restricted groups ask that you subscribe before viewing postings.

How to subscribe

Click on the name of the group you want to join. This should give you a summary of the last few postings that have appeared, to give you a feel for the types of things being discussed.

• Click on **Subscribe to this group**.

If you are on Google groups, then you will be asked for your Google account. One of the other advantages of having an account is the Google bookmark (or favourites) facility, so you can access any link you have added whether you are on your own machine or any other in, say, a library.

• Click **Create an account now** and you will be taken to another page to fill in your e-mail address, choose a password and a nickname.

Sign in with your
Google **Account**

Email:

Password:

☑ Remember me on this computer.

Sign in

I cannot access my account

You may be asking why you might want a nickname rather than just your own name. If you need one, is it really safe to be subscribing? Well, like many things, it is always better to be safe than sorry. Anyone can tell you anything about themselves and sadly there are a few unscrupulous people who might use your details if they were given more information. Don't let this frighten you off, though. In the many years I have been using the internet, I have never run into any problems. But take sensible precautions. For instance, I would recommend that women pick a gender-free nickname and one that makes no reference to them or their family.

- Once you have completed all the boxes, click on **I accept**.

Create an account

Your Google Account gives you access to Google Groups and other Google services. If you already have a Google Account, you can sign in here.

Required information for Google account

Your current email address:

e.g. myname@example.com. This will be used to sign-in to your account.

Choose a password: Password strength:

Minimum of 8 characters in length.

Re-enter password:

☑ Remember me on this computer.

Creating a Google Account will enable Web History. Web History is a feature that will provide you with a more personalised experience on Google that includes more relevant search results and recommendations. Learn More
☑ Enable Web History.

You will be taken to a new page. An e-mail will be sent to the address you have given to ensure that you verify this is the correct address. This is simply part of the security of the site, so that the moderators can crack down on fraudsters and spammers who try to get into these groups. You can safely open this e-mail and verify your account by clicking on the link in the message. You will be ready to proceed to the group or groups that you are interested in.

- Once you have verified your account, click on **Manage account profile** and then on **Groups**.

I recommend typing in the subject you are looking for, rather than going through all the lists.

Looking at postings

Having chosen your group and opened your Google account, you will be redirected to the page to set up your options.

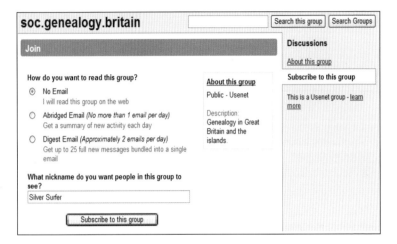

As you can see, you can choose how and when you view newsgroups. If you just want to look at them on the web as and when you want, then the 'no e-mail' option will suit you. If you want to know what is happening, and whether people are posting subjects that might interest you, then the 'abridged e-mail' will suit you. If you want a synopsis of what is being posted then the 'digest e-mail' will be best. Of course, the last two options will only help if you check your e-mail!

Don't worry if you change your mind

If the group you subscribed to isn't what you expected, you can simply unsubscribe (see page 81).

Look at the message here: this is a posting from a newsgroup, and tells us several things. Firstly who posted it (you will get to know regular posters on groups that you subscribe to), what time they posted it and how many replies the post has got.

• To read the replies, click on **Expand all** (or similar) and you will be able to see what other people are saying on this matter. The messages will start with the original post, and then in time or date order of the replies.

Posting a reply

Posting a reply or a new topic on a newsgroup is very similar to sending a regular e-mail.

• Click on **Reply group** and type in your comment.

• Click on **Send**.

Remember: anybody can see this message and who sent it. If you want to send a private reply i.e. just to the person raising the question, then click on **Reply**. Be aware, however, that many people disguise their e-mail address by putting gaps or spelling the word AT instead of the symbol @ to try and stop spam.

If you want to post on a new subject (and have checked that it does not already exist), most groups have a 'New Post' or 'Post New Subject' button. All you have to do is click on that, follow the golden rules on page 83 and on you go.

Looking at newsgroups using Outlook Express

It is also possible to look at newsgroups using your normal e-mail program.

- Open Outlook Express as if you were going to read or send an e-mail. Click on **Tools**.

- Click on **Accounts**.

- When the window opens, click on **News**.

- Then click on **Add**.

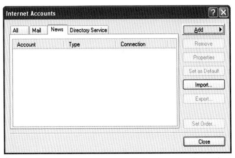

A box will appear for you to complete your details, very much like the one for e-mail. You will need to know the details of your ISP's news server to access the list, for instance 'news.virgin.net'.

- Click on **Finish** and then **Close**. A window will pop up, asking whether you want to download newsgroups from the server. This means that you will get a complete list of all the available groups (not that you will have subscribed to them!).

Once they have finished downloading, a window will be on your screen showing an alphabetical (and quite possibly long) list of groups. I have always found that to get the best idea of what the groups are about it is helpful to tick the box for searching descriptions. However, you should be aware of two things: firstly, the groups will have to reload, so if it took a long time first time round you may wish to forgo this step; secondly, not all groups bother putting a description, so you will not get information on all the groups.

- To find a group that suits your needs, type in the search box underneath 'Display newsgroups that contain' and the list will either display matches or, if there are no matches, it will tell you so.

- If you find a group that you like the look of, click on **Subscribe** and then on **Go to**.

This will put the group in your folder list under newsgroups, and will download any messages that have been posted, usually in date order. Messages with replies (or threads) will have a plus sign next to them.

- Click on **+** and the messages will expand, showing you all the replies as they were posted.

To unsubscribe

If you decide the group is not for you or that no one else is bothering with it, you can unsubscribe.

- Click on the name of the newsgroup server in your folder list and then on newsgroups in the pane to the right of this.

- In the new window click on **Subscribed** to see a list of groups to which you have signed up.

- Click on the name of the group you wish to leave. Click on **Unsubscribe**. This will take you off the list, and remove any postings from your e-mail program.

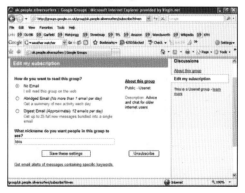

All that jargon

As you are reading the newsgroups you may notice some abbreviations, similar to those we discussed earlier regarding textspeak (see page 44). Here are some of the more popular ones; memorise these and not only will you look like a seasoned poster, but you might even impress the youngsters!

- **AFAIK:** As far as I know

- **AIUI:** As I understand it

- **BTW:** By the way

- **C&C:** Coffee and cats, meaning 'put your coffee in a safe place and shoo the cat off your lap before you ROTFL (see below)

- **FAQ:** Frequently asked question

- **HAND:** Have a nice day

- **HTH:** Hope this helps

- **IANAL:** I am not a lawyer

- **IIRC:** If I recall correctly

- **IMHO:** In my humble opinion

- **IOW:** In other words

- **LOL:** Laughs out loud

- **OTOH:** On the other hand

- **OT:** Off topic

- **RFC:** Request for comments

- **RFD:** Request for discussion

- **ROTFL:** Roll on the floor laughing.

I am sure there are others (and you could always invent a few).

Some guidelines on posting

Before you start posting, take some time to look at what other people are saying, how they say it and any abbreviations that may be used. Look at some of the older messages and make sure that no one else has already posted or replied on the subject you want to raise.

A very important rule to remember is that people don't always phrase themselves exactly as they mean. It is easy to take offence or misinterpret comments that are made on the internet; bear in mind that people can't see that tongue in your cheek as you type away on your computer!

Remember: what you say on a newsgroup can be read by millions of people all over the world, so if someone annoys you, or you disagree with their opinion don't get into a virtual slanging match with them. It is always possible they didn't actually mean what you thought they meant. If you can't agree or you really dislike their opinion, don't read their postings.

When you decide the time is ready for you to post, either as a new post or a reply, follow these basic rules:

- Do not give out personal information, such as your address.

- Keep it brief – say what you need to say and leave it at that.

- Make sure your posting title tells the other group members exactly what you are posting. People often belong to many groups and will skim-read the titles to check if they really want to read the message.

- Make sure your posting is relevant to the group you are posting to. (Asking about stamp collecting on a heavy metal enthusiasts' group might get you answers you weren't expecting!)

- Be careful with humour. People can't tell if you are joking when they can't see you.

- Before you reply, make sure you are not repeating what someone else has just said.

- There are groups that are designed specifically for advertising. Use them if you are selling something, and not one of the groups for discussion.

Finally, remember that you will probably never meet any of your group members, and their knowledge of you will be from your postings. Make sure that this reflects who you are.

Chapter 6

Bulletins and Blogs

A look at message boards or forums follows on naturally from newsgroups. You might wonder what the difference is between forums and groups, as they look very similar and behave in a similar way.

Simply put, a message board or forum is usually on one specific subject with comments posted chronologically or as conversation threads. A thread is an ongoing conversation on one particular subject or aspect of a subject. It can go on for as long or as short a time as the board members wish; a member could add a comment to it months after it was originally posted, if he or she thought it was relevant.

There is a vast array of boards on a huge amount of subjects. On the whole, the main difference with boards is that you need to check them rather than them e-mailing content or advising you of posts, although some boards do now e-mail content as well. Message boards can be informative and quite lively, depending on the subject matter!

Message boards

Try **www.lifeoutloud.co.uk**, a website aimed at 'the wiser generation'. It has a number of message boards.

Subjects under each category cover all manner of topics (and, I have to say, some of the worst jokes I have seen in a long while!). As with the newsgroups, especially the more diverse ones, it is worth having a wander around to see what the topics are, and the tone of those posting to the boards.

You are now viewing all topics		
Daily Chat Last updated: 13/11/2007 12:33:18	Replies: 8	By: lacemaker
Todays quiz question Last updated: 13/11/2007 12:31:15	Replies: 1700	By: lacemaker
Welcome to the new site! Last updated: 11/11/2007 07:23:27	Replies: 3	By: Rosebud
WORD ASSOCIATION Last updated: 10/11/2007 18:28:36	Replies: 6769	By: lacemaker
POETRY Last updated: 9/11/2007 07:13:30	Replies: 0	By: kaliavijay2003
VERSE Last updated: 9/11/2007 05:47:05	Replies: 1	By: kaliavijay2003

Another site worth visiting is **www.50connect.co.uk/ 50cforums/** with its motto 'Live life to the full', where the message boards range from technology to nostalgia and many things in between. Similar in content is **www.mapleand leek.com**: 'Live it up at 50+. Adventures starts here.'

These sites all need you to register to contribute, but not to read. Although that sounds a little irksome just imagine what could, and no doubt would, appear on the boards if anyone could post. Try looking at a few guest books on websites that are not well maintained; they amass spam postings each day.

Blogs

Well, it has been on the news and they all appear to be doing it, from the kids to the politicians and many in between. But what is blogging?

The word blog is short for web log, which is essentially an online diary or journal created by someone to record in writing their thoughts, feelings or views on either a specific subject or life in general. Usually appearing in chronological order, a blog can be informative, amusing and often contentious (and sometimes quite tedious). It can contain photographs, cartoons or just text. It can also often have links to other websites or blogs – either on similar subjects, or just liked by the blogger and recommended to anyone interested.

Many blogs invite, in fact positively encourage, readers to leave a comment on the page, which can also be seen by anyone visiting the site. This whole interactive, fast-changing, 'anything goes' sort of approach makes it a fascinating, if slightly bewildering mode of expression. At the time of writing, figures showed that a search engine that specifically tracked blogs was close to showing one hundred million blogs across the world, and no doubt this will have increased many times by the time I have finished this page.

There are a variety of blogs available, and they have their own names depending on their speciality or even how they actually got to be on the web in the first place. For instance:

- A blog comprising videos is called a vlog

- A site containing a portfolio of sketches is called a sketchblog

- One comprising photos is called a photoblog

- An artlog is a form of art sharing and publishing in the format of a blog, but relies mainly on showing artwork rather than text.

Blogs are also named for the way in which they are transmitted to the web, e.g. a blog sent from a mobile phone or a PDA is called a moblog.

There are many blogs on the web, and you could spend all day wandering through them. One of my favourites is www.allaboutolive.com.au or 'The Life of Riley' as the title of the page goes.

Olive Riley was born on 20 October 1899 – yes, I did say *1899* – and is believed to be the world's oldest blogger (or 'blobber' as she calls it). Strictly speaking, she actually dictates the contents and someone else enters it on to the blog, but I am not going to quibble. In this context, blogging is really a new take on an old form of oral history and means that memories can be preserved that would otherwise be lost forever.

I can also recommend **www.sammsville.com** for a tale of a British couple and their family, travels and life in general, not to mention some superb photography.

Creating your blog

So, you have seen all these e-scribblings and thought to yourself: 'I could do that'. Perhaps your children or grandchildren have asked you to tell them a bit about what it was like growing up, or maybe you just want to get something off your chest.

There are a number of sites that will allow you to create your own, including the example here, Blogger.

- From Internet Explorer, go to **https://www2.blogger.com/ start**.

- Click on **Create your blog now**.

- Sign in using your Google account (see page 76).

- Type in a user name. This is the name you will use to access your blog whenever you want to add or edit it.

- Check the box to confirm you have read the terms and conditions, then click on **Continue**.

- Type in a name for your blog and check its availability.

This is where you need to have a bit of thought. If your blog is on a very specific subject, then it would be best to ensure the name reflects that. Calling a blog 'Under Milkwood' for instance, and then going on to have nothing to do with Dylan Thomas or even any of the cast of any film or radio version of the book would be likely to cause great confusion. If your blog is a general 'thoughts on' or 'recollections of' I would suggest you include that, and if it is on a particular place also include that. Have a look on the blog searches for other blogs that include any of the description you might like, to make sure you are not going to get confused with someone else.

- Click on **Continue** to go to the next window.

- Next choose a template, then click on **Continue**.

Bear in mind, some people have problems reading text on a dark background; others don't like a website that they feel is too busy. If in doubt, keep it simple and look for the design that you would find easy to look at. You can change the template later if you want to.

Posting on your blog

Now comes the exciting part. You are ready to share your thoughts with the world!

• Click on **Start posting**.

To begin with, it is a good idea to tell people a little bit about yourself and why you are writing a blog. Then start the subject you feel you want to blog on.

When you have finished typing, it is a good idea to see what it will look like before you send it out into the world. It is amazing how you are more likely to spot an error, or want to change a word when you get to this stage, even though you have read and re-read the original many times.

• Click on **Preview** up in the top right-hand corner.

Look at my blog in preview:

You can see that I have added a title and, more importantly, some labels. These are important as they enable search engines to pick up your site when someone asks for a specific subject. If I went to Google blog search and asked for blogs on silver surfers, I hope that mine would come up. The important thing with labels or keywords is to ensure that they cover the various things on the site, and are likely to fall under a wide umbrella search. When you are looking for something, you might not always know exactly what it is called or what you want, so a broad search will pick up your site if it is labelled correctly.

- Once you are sure the content is right, the title is right and the labels are done, click on **Publish post** – and you are now the proud owner of a blog.

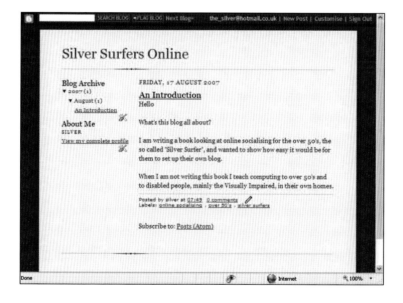

Following up

Having posted your first blog, what comes next? Well, unless you don't really have that much to say, you will want to go back into your blog to add comments, look to see if anyone else has added a comment or possibly just to edit what you have put on there.

When you set up your blog, you created an address. (In my example, this was http://silversurfersonline.blogspot.com.)

- Open Internet Explorer and in the address bar, type the address you created.

- Click on **Go** to load the web page.

- Once your blog page has opened, click on **Sign in**.

If you are using your own computer I would suggest putting a tick in the box for Remember me, but never do this on a public computer.

- Type in the e-mail address and password you registered with, and log in.

Once your blog page has opened, you should have the option to edit your page or create a new post. You will be blogging like a professional in no time!

After a while, people should start to see your blog (especially if you tell them about it) and they can post a comment to your page. Visitors to your blog can leave a message to say if they agree or disagree with something you have said, or just to say whether they like it.

The more people who visit your blog and leave comments or tell their friends by sending links to it, the livelier it will get. If you do have a story to tell or a point to make, you should start reaching a good audience.

The really important thing about a good blog is to keep adding to it on a regular basis. If people get into the habit of visiting it because there is always something new to read or look at then you should gain a faithful audience. If, however, you go for weeks or months without bothering to post anything, you will find yourself all alone.

Video blogging

Take inspiration from **www.askgeriatric.com**. Born in 1927, Peter Oakley is one of the most viewed contributors to You Tube (**http://uk.youtube.com/**), a video site where members of the public can send videos for other people to enjoy.

The headline on You Tube is 'Broadcast yourself' and many people do take this quite literally! There are some great video clips on there, some from people mucking about at home, some from people who have obviously spent hours creating a short film (I love the Lego ones myself), some of pets doing weird and wonderful things and some with a social or political comment to make.

If you want to post a video to You Tube, you will need to create an account exactly the same as any other registration.

- From Internet Explorer, go to www.youtube.com.

- Fill in your personal details on the form on the right of the screen. For now, opt for a Standard account.

- Click **Sign up**.

- You will be sent a verification e-mail. Confirm your e-mail address by clicking on the link within the message and go to your account.

- Click on **Upload new video** (you may have to reconfirm your e-mail address) and finally you will get to the video upload page.

- Give your video a title, something that will draw people to look at it.

- Add a brief description to give people an idea what it is all about.

- Choose which section would best suit its contents: comedy, news and politics, etc. The site automatically assumes that you want to share your video with the public.

- Finally, click on **Upload a video**.

- Browse to find the video on your computer, then click on **Upload video**.

Depending on the size of the video, uploading it might take a few minutes. Once it finishes uploading and has been processed by the site, that's it: you are a broadcasting star!

 Don't worry about uploading

Uploading is the opposite of downloading, i.e., you are transferring something from your computer to a website.

For a list of all the blogs available on the BBC (and you would be surprised how many there are), go to: **www.bbc.co.uk/blogs** where you will find delights such as 'Blether with Brian', the excellent Ouch blog from the BBC disability show and a wealth of links to local BBC blogs.

To find a blog that interests you try **www.britblog.com** or **www.google.co.uk/blogsearch**. Just enter a brief description (in the same way as any search) and see what is out there.

One of the most popular blog search engines is **http://technorati.com/** and here you can search under many things, but for sheer idle curiosity try clicking on 'Popular' just to see what other people are looking at.

Chapter 7

Social Networking Sites

It is difficult to know exactly when social networking sites came into being. There are those who say that they are a continuation of the social networks created on dating sites, and then expanded to a wider audience. Certainly, there has been some form of networking via newsgroups or user groups since the late 1990s.

The general opinion is that the incarnation of this type of site was 'born' in 2003 when a site called Friendster (**www.friend ster.com**) was created. Friendster boasts more than 48 million members worldwide, and is aimed at helping adults stay in touch with friends, family, school, groups, activities and interests, and to discover new people and things that are important to them. Based in San Francisco, the site is one of the first of many to spring up aimed at allowing and encouraging people to maintain or create contact with others, no matter where in the world they are.

There has been a huge increase in social networking sites and the number of people who use them. Some figures show over 70% growth on the more popular sites between 2006 and 2007. It seems that almost anyone who is anyone has a MySpace or Facebook entry, but what are they?

A social networking site is a combination of things all put together in one place. It will normally consist of some blogs, some groups, some messaging, some chat facilities and also file or photo sharing. The idea is to get together online communities of people to communicate with one another. Some sites started off as groups of people with a similar interest or background, and developed into larger groups with many different interests.

There still remain sites dedicated entirely to a common interest, e.g., genealogy, music or books, but most of the popular sites are varied and have groups within them. There are also groups that have got together due to their shared like (or dislike) of a certain thing or even sometimes person. There are even groups who have got together due to a shared last name, not a genealogy group but just a social group spread around the world.

The main purpose of a networking site is to build up a community, whether that be of friends you already have in your Address book (the site can check your Address book if you have certain types of webmail, to see if anyone you have listed also has a Facebook account) or friends you acquire.

There are various ways to acquire these friends, one of which is to share friends with other friends. For instance, a friend you have in your Address book may have a pal you have never met, but who has similar interests to you. By putting you in contact with them on a networking site, you can communicate, even if you are on different continents.

You can also add friends from groups that you join, if you want to carry on talking to them outside of the group. Most networking sites will let you know if someone from your list of friends is online at the same time as you are.

If you have a friend in your list, you can see what groups they join, when and if they post a comment or a photograph and which friends they add to their list. Occasionally, you might find mutual friends that you did not know had a profile – in which case you can 'poke' them. This is the equivalent of a Messenger nudge or a wink and is a way of bringing your friend's attention to your presence on Facebook, without adding them to your list.

Top networking sites

The top sites at present appear to be MySpace (**www.myspace.com**), Facebook (**www.facebook.com**) and Bebo (**www.bebo.com**). Although they may appear to be slightly youth orientated, they are increasingly drawing older participants. Personally, I find Facebook a more restful site with a clean feel to it and less visually distracting stimuli, but they will all do similar things.

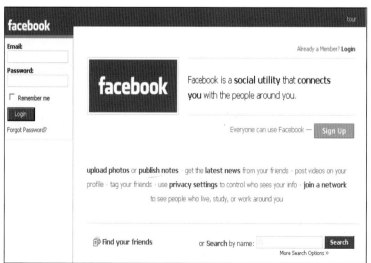

There are a number of groups on Facebook created and contributed to by various age groups, including the over 50s. It is an interesting and lively place for social networking, but it also has a more serious side as political parties and lobbying groups start to use it to get their messages across. Facebook has also been praised in the press for the speed with which it responds to complaints about postings that do not conform to its code of practice.

Bebo is increasingly drawing more young people who want to move away from MySpace, but it is very much a fluid thing with some groups moving back and forth.

The figures for membership on these sites are huge, but it is believed that many people sign up and keep on board for a while, and then drift away, either to another site or because they just lose interest (or the time to do it).

Saga Zone

Late in 2007, Saga, a company that specialises in products and publications for the over 50s, joined the social networking trend by creating Saga Zone.

Saga Zone (**www.sagazone.co.uk**) is a site like Facebook, Bebo and My Space, but with one very important difference: it only accepts the over 50s! Although all the other sites have no age limit (in either direction) and many have groups specifically aimed at the older social networker, they are often perceived as something for the teens.

Saga Zone has all the features of the other sites but none of the gadgets, gizmos and sometimes silliness that they suffer from.

Registration is free, and at the time of writing this, there were over 27,000 people registered, even though it had only been open a few months. Once registered, you are called upon to create a profile

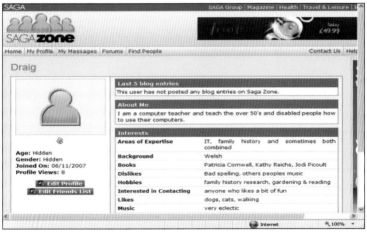

As you can see from the image above, questions are sensible and ensure that you have a good chance of being contacted by someone with similar interests. In fact, within days of being registered, I was sent a link to a lovely site for walks. The site also has a clean, easy-to-navigate feel to it.

Saga Zone Forums

The forums are organised into specific subjects and this makes it easy to find topics that interest you or just to browse to get the feel of it.

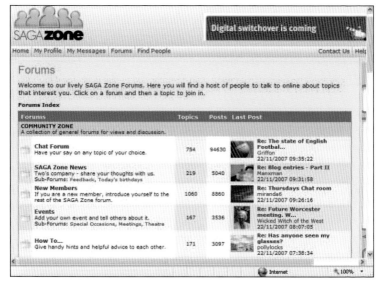

Topics on the forums range from general chat to health to technology and recipes. There is also an entire section for events, which seems to be lively and well used, where people can suggest or organise meetings with people either with similar interests or living in the same area.

As with any forum, I would always advise taking the time to look at the various postings, have a look at other people's profiles and see whether you could improve the details that you have given, and generally take your time to get to know the site.

Most of the times I have been on the site there have been up to 200 people online at differing times of the day and evening. One of the really important things I have noticed about this site is that not only does everyone seem friendly, but also they seem eager to help with queries and suggestions, tips on using the posts and where to look for things.

Other sites to try

Eons (http://eons.com): dedicated particularly to older users, with the slogan 'Lovin' life on the flip side of 50'. It was created by the founder of **www.monster.com**, which is an incredibly popular job search site (see page 145).

Eons is quite a big site, but at the moment appears to be mainly American, so may lack reference points for UK users. For instance, most of its obituaries (81 million last time I looked) seem to be US based. However, it does have some good features, games and articles and some interesting groups, so will be worth keeping an eye on.

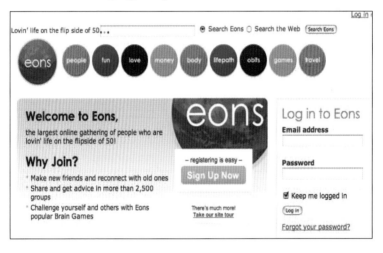

Geni (www.geni.com): dedicated to genealogy, under the banner 'Everyone's related'. If you want to join this free site, all you have to do is enter your name and your parents' names (and more if you know it) and your account is created.

IVillage (www.ivillage.co.uk): for women networkers (sorry, gents). Billing itself as a community website it focuses on 'the issues that matter most to women and offers interactive services, expert advice, information and a vital support network'. Subjects covered on the site include diet and fitness,

relationships, parenting, pregnancy and baby, health, beauty, food and drink, home and garden, travel, money, news and entertainment, work and career, and astrology. There is also a free networking section very similar to Facebook, with profiles, photos and even blogs for those that want them. It all looks very cosy and may not be to everyone's tastes, and there does appear to be rather an emphasis on parenthood and parenting. However, that said, there are groups, boards and information pages galore and it does not appear to be the haunt of teenagers so it definitely has its up side.

Flickr (www.flickr.com): if writing is not necessarily your thing, but you do a bit of photography, then this might be the place for you. Originally a sort of holding bay for photographs where people could share their photographs with anyone over the world, it has migrated into almost a photo journal site. Many blog sites link back to this one, in order to allow people reading the blogs to see photographs to accompany the article. There is also a recent addition to the Flickr site for blogging.

Twitter (http://twitter.com): one of the strangest sites I have come across. Its slogan is 'A global community of friends and strangers answering one simple question: *What are you doing?'* From what I have seen each time I have visited, it seems to consist of people constantly updating the world with the minutiae of their daily lives, either by web, text or IM. Comments posted include things like 'walking the dog', or 'sitting in a traffic jam' and are written in whatever language is relevant to the poster. There is also a tie between Facebook and Twitter, so I assume that you can post 'writing in Facebook' and it will appear on Twitter. I have the feeling that I am probably missing something as far as this particular website is concerned!

Dogster and Catster (www.dogster.com and www.catster.com): two sites that delight me for their sheer improbability. Yes, you have guessed right: they are social networking sites for pets. These are American sites launched during 2004, and between them they boast a staggering three million photos for over 450,000 uploaded pets by 500,000 members. The two sites supply more than 22 million pages a month to over three-quarters of a million visitors. If you are a pet lover then they are definitely worth a look. They are fun, cute – possibly a little too cute at times – and work well.

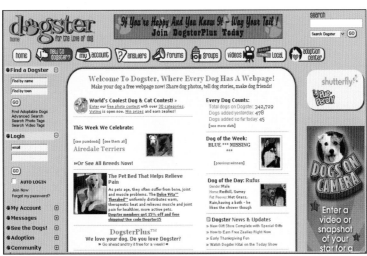

You may also want to look at **www.livejournal.com** or **http://spaces.live.com** from Windows or **http://360.yahoo.com**.

There is a really nice feel to some of these sites. People are genuinely friendly, and looking to expand their friendships rather than getting on a soapbox, and I would recommend having a look around one or two of them to find out what the tone is on different groups.

Joining a networking site

All sites require you to register, and most are free. When you register on a site like these, you create a profile giving people some information about yourself, such as where you live (though not your actual address), your age, and what you like or don't like. As with newsgroups, if after joining you decide that you don't like the content, you can always leave. You can also belong to more than one group at a time.

Using Google or other search engine, search for List of social networking sites, and then refine your search further by using a keyword such as 50 (or anything else that might interest you). Take a look at some of the sites you find. You may like to visit Facebook. Once you are on the site, you can search for groups such as "over 50' and you may find something like this.

Group:	AAAAAAAAge over 50.....I know you're out there	View Group
Network:	Global	Join Group
Size:	262 members	
Type:	Just for Fun - Facebook Classics	
New:	3 Fewer Members	

What this will tell you is the name of the group, whether it is worldwide (global) or based in one particular country, how many people belong to the group and the reason for the group: in this example, just for fun – which sounds good enough to me! One of the joys of a site like Facebook is that it is truly global. There are postings from around the world, including the UK, USA, Australia, United Arab Emirates and Norway.

Chapter 8

Games and Hobbies

You may at this point be wondering quite how you can go tenpin bowling or horse riding on the computer, and obviously the answer is you can't! But you *can* use your computer to look up where you can do these and many other things for real.

There are many websites that are either specifically aimed at hobbies, or have a section on hobbies as part of their forums, so it is always worth having a look at these to see if there is anyone with similar interests. For instance, **www.hobbyworld united.com** is aimed at people discussing their pastimes, and below you will see a list of some of the hobbies – no doubt this will increase as more people join.

Hobbies Menu

Jump into the wonderful world of hobbies
Just choose a hobby from the list below and start to explore the hidden treasures that make Hobbyworldunited the best place on the internet for hobbyists.

Antiques	Knitting
Art	Lace Making
Astrology	Literature
Astronomy	Metal Detecting
Card Making	Model Engineering
Clock Making	Patchwork/Quilting
Collecting	Photography
Computing	Pottery/Ceramics
Cooking	Radio Control
Crochet	Rubber Stamping
Cross Stitching	Scrapbooking
Dolls House Making	Sewing
Fish Keeping	Teddybears
Fishing/Angling	Upholstery/Soft Furnishing
Gardening	Walking
Genealogy	Water Activities
Hat Making	Wood Working
Jewellery/Beading	

Not only can you talk about your hobbies, but you can also ask questions of other enthusiasts, find out whether there are any national or local clubs, and get news of any upcoming events, such as collectors' fairs. Many clubs get significant discounts for their members, so it is worth keeping an eye open for these.

What's on near you?

One of the great advantages of the internet is that you can join in from the comfort of your home with a group anywhere in the world. However, if you are looking for groups that exist in your area, with a view to getting out and enjoying some activities or taking up a new hobby, then **www.direct.gov.uk/en/** is a good place to start looking.

This is part of a government website that covers all age groups, but has excellent facilities for finding out information on all manner of things.

- From Internet Explorer, go to www.direct.gov.uk/en/ and click on **Over 50s**.

- In section entitled Travel and Leisure, click on **Leisure** and a new page will open:

> **Over 50s**
>
> ## Leisure
>
> **Work the way you want**
> Do you want to change how you work? Find out about becoming self-employed, working reduced hours, volunteering and your rights under the age discrimination laws
>
> ▸ Working to suit you for over 50s

- Click on **Find out** to discover more about leisure activities for older people.

In the new window you can search for activities by postcode, street or town or by your local authority.

- Enter your choice, then click on **Go** and you will be redirected to a page dealing specifically with your area.

It is also worth looking at your local council website to see whether they have any activities specifically aimed at older people: **www.*yourtown*.gov.uk**. Now could be your ideal time to take up a hobby you have previously only dreamed of: what about dance classes, painting or aqua aerobics or even learning to swim? Your local leisure centre may also run events and most places have a website to check it out. Many councils also offer free or subsidised keep fit classes for over 50s, so they could be a great way to stay trim and meet new people.

Websites for walkers

Walking is an ideal way to take a regular, safe and achievable form of exercise. It is good for your heart, helps to control your weight and blood pressure, and is good for your bones. Walking on your own can be pleasant, but I admit that if I did not have a dog I probably would not go half the time. The solution to this is to join a group.

Walking the Way to Health (www.whi.org.uk): a national initiative spearheaded by Natural England and the British Heart Foundation. The project provides local walking opportunities to walk in company, led by trained volunteers, aimed at encouraging people aged 50+ who need to exercise for health reasons. Walking the Way to Health has helped to create over 400 local health walk schemes and has trained over 30,000 volunteer walk leaders. Since 2000, it is estimated that the project has encouraged over a million people to walk more. The website will show whether there is a walk near you.

Ramblers Association (www.ramblers.org.uk): if you would like something possibly a little more strenuous, the Ramblers Association has over 500 groups throughout the UK. Use this website to check to see if there is one near you. There is also a message board for people to use to find walking companions, so if you have your heart set on walking up Snowdon but don't fancy it on your own, this is the place to go.

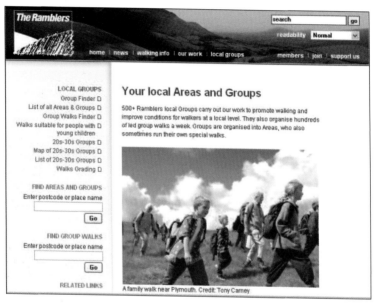

A family walk near Plymouth. Credit: Tony Carney

Ramblers Holidays (www.ramblersholidays.co.uk): if you want more exercise or a break that does not involve lying on a beach somewhere, a walking holiday might be the answer.

Walking for the disabled (www.disabledramblers.co.uk or in Scotland **www.ftdr.com):** if you would love to go get out into the countryside, but are not all that mobile, try Disabled Ramblers. This group uses a variety of mobility aids ranging from electrically powered pavement buggies, scooters, power chairs and, in some cases, manually propelled wheelchairs to travel paths and trails in the country. It organises supported rambles of varying difficulty all over England and Wales, or Scotland, and each event provides recreation and challenge to suit most tastes. Rambles have included places such as the New Forest, the Thames path, North Yorkshire Moors and the Gower Peninsula, and vary from easy, where the surface is level, to challenging, which will be uneven, with some steep gradients and probably a rocky surface. The distance covered is usually about eight miles. Rambles are open to members only (although they are happy to let you go on one to see how you enjoy it) and there are heavy-duty scooters available for loan on a first-come basis.

Transportdirect

Not everybody drives or wants to drive to some places. Transport Direct (**www.transportdirect.info**) is a site that helps you make your travel arrangements by telling you how long the journey will take and what your options are. Now, you might note that this is a slightly strange web address, in that it ends in 'info' rather than any of the standard domains. This is because it is a non-profit consortium run by, among others, the Department of Transport, with information from all the major rail, coach and bus operators.

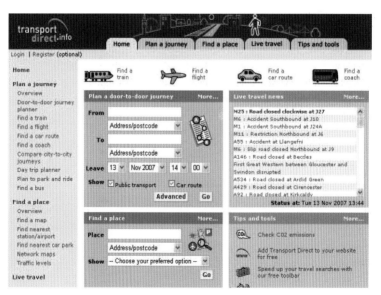

Transportdirect is particularly useful as it will compare car and public transport journeys, so you can work out which is quicker or easier. It will also tell you which station you will need at both ends.

Having planned your journey, the site also has live traffic and travel updates, so you can see whether the road you are travelling on has any jams, or the train has delays due to points failure or the wrong sort of leaves on the track.

If you are using public transport, you can book your ticket via the site. It has links to the bus and train companies and will either issue you with an 'e-ticket' that you get by e-mail and print out to take with you on the day, or you can collect your ticket from the station before you go.

If you do decide to drive (and assuming you haven't invested in satnav), you can get a detailed route either from this site or the AA (**www.theaa.com**) or the RAC (**www.rac.co.uk**).

Online societies

If this all sounds a bit exhausting (and I'm worn out just looking it up myself), what about joining an online society?

These are similar to the social networking sites discussed in Chapter 7, but the main aim of them is further an interest, rather than socialising (although this may well be a spin-off of your involvement). Use your search engine to find, for example, local history society online. This will suggest links, such as **www.local-history.co.uk** that you can then pursue. Alternatively, if you already belong to a society, it is worth checking to see if there is an online community that you could join. Go to the main website of your chosen organisation for more information.

Website **www.50connect.co.uk** is also a useful combination of boards, information and chat, as well as some special offers.

LOCAL HISTORY ONLINE

Calendar

Latest news

Latest issue

Past issues

Bookshop

Getting started

History into Print

Welcome to **Local History Online**, one of the UK's premier sites for local history, with over 300 links to sites both in the UK and overseas, regularly updated News and Calendar sections, directories of local history organisations and course providers and an on-line Bookshop, with stock at discounted prices.

The Local History Bookshop

The Bookshop has been expanded, so now you can buy a selection of local history books and Historical Association pamphlets, as well as take out a subscription to *Local History Magazine* or buy all the back issues which are still in print. Payment by credit/debit card is completely secure. If you prefer to pay by cheque, or wish to place an official order, then please download our Booklist (5-page pdf file), which you will need Acrobat

LocalHistory

Local History Magazine, the UK's only independent national magazine for anyone with an interest in local history, was

Online games

Bridge (www.bridgeclublive.com): fancy a game of bridge but no one to play with? This is an online bridge site that has been operating since 1994, has thousands of members throughout the world and is an English Bridge Union (EBU) affiliated club. It holds regular online tournaments and offers coaching. This is a paid-for site, but it offers a 30-day trial membership to let you get a feel for how it operates, and allows you into a main room and offers some coaching.

If you enjoy bridge and want to build up a group to play with regularly, they also have a 'friends' system where you can see when people in your list come online. As it is worldwide (when I last looked there were about 150 people on from 24 countries), there should be someone available for a game or conversation, whatever time of the day or night you decide to join in.

Chess (www.freechess.org): boasts over 300,000 registered users and offers games at various levels. Also try **www.letsplaychess.com** with over 450,000 members and the chance to participate in tournaments, **www.worldchess live.com**, **www.chessclub.com** and **www.chesshere.com**

Some online clubs want you to register but have no fee, but some do charge. I would suggest that you check which of these does before you register. If all you want is the odd game, then probably a completely free site would suit you. If, however, you are quite serious about your chess, you may want to subscribe to one of the paid-for clubs.

Backgammon (www.gammonempire.com or **www.play 65.com/index.html):** both these sites appear to be looking at betting on ongoing games, but there are a number of sites with games being played for fun. For example, **www.nabisco world.com/games** has backgammon, ping-pong, marbles, mah-jongg and many other games. Be warned, though: you could get hooked!

Gambling: if you fancy a flutter, figures are showing that online poker is a hugely growing phenomenon with revenue figures in the range of billions of dollars. Try one of the following sites:

- www.coralpoker.com
- www.empirepoker.com
- www.ladbrokespoker.com
- www.littlewoodspoker.com
- www.pacificpoker.com
- www.planetpoker.com

In the UK most of the major bookmakers have online betting facilities, so if you do like a bet you can log on and create an account. Try William Hill (**www.willhill.com**) or Coral (**www.coral.co.uk**).

You can even play bingo online. Go to **www.onlinebingo.co.uk** to find out more about sites that are available, what the prizes are and what is being recommended at the moment.

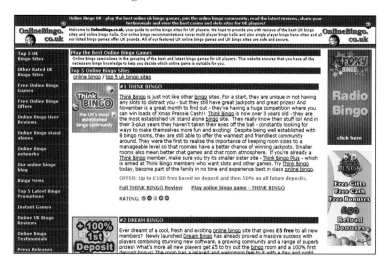

Jigsaws (www.jigzone.com): Want to amuse yourself for an hour or two but not necessarily in a competitive way? Why not try doing a jigsaw online. It is quite addictive, and you can choose not only the picture but also how many pieces and even the pattern it is cut into. The good news is it can't have a piece missing and you don't have to put it away in the box when you have finished (and the cat can't walk across it and knock it on the floor!).

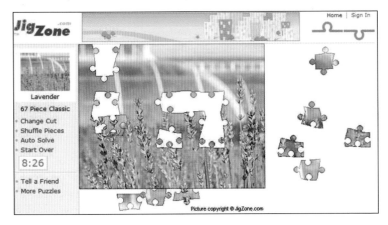

For online games in general try:

- **www.aarp.org/fun/puzzles/**

- **http://games.yahoo.com/games/front**

- **www.shockwave.com/home.jsp**

Many of the newsgroup or general forum sites also have some great games, including Scrabble, sudoku and some word games to keep the old grey matter active.

Ebooks

An electronic book or ebook is like a conventional printed book that you can read either on your computer or have read to you via a piece of software called an ebook reader.

In 2000, the well-known and prodigious writer Stephen King released a 66-page story as an ebook. Within hours the queues of people trying to download it were so big that the servers (the computer it was stored on) dealing with it crashed! Not many modern popular authors are publishing in this way, and Mr King himself says that the printed book is still very much alive and kicking. However, it is comparable to audio books, where there is a certain charm and joy to having a story read to you. If also you have visual problems, or find reading tiring or difficult, what could be nicer than a soothing tale?

Admittedly, some of the software for ebook readers has an air of robot about it, but not all do. I would recommend investigating Microsoft Reader, which is free and can be downloaded from **www.microsoft.com/reader/downloads/ pc.mspx**. It will read for you – and even keeps your place when you stop it.

Not all books are available for ebook download, and not all books are compatible with Reader. However, many of the classics are (copyright laws play not a little part in this).

I am very fond of **http://esspc-ebooks.com/all.asp**, having spent many an hour teaching a blind student to use this, so she could reread all the books from her youth. Here you will find Charles Dickens, Jane Austen, George Eliot and many others.

There are many sites on the internet that you can download ebooks from, but be aware that many of them charge for downloading on a per item basis (think of it as buying a book from a bookseller).

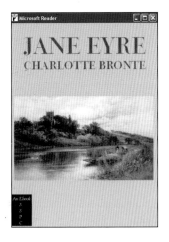

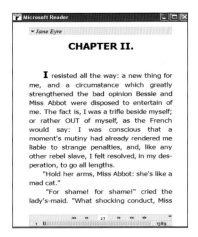

Many ebooks are also available for use on PDAs, which have the advantage of being smaller to carry with you and can contain several books at a time. Obviously, you are unlikely to take a desktop computer on holiday with you (or even to bed to read), but a PDA fits in your hand or bag.

Online book groups

If you enjoy reading, and would like to share your experience with others or would like to discuss reviews, why not join a book club? As you can imagine, there are a number of these on the internet, working very like the newsgroups we looked at in Chapter 6.

There are two types of ebook clubs online. The first type is members clubs for buying and downloading ebooks. There are a number of these available on the internet, and they are similar to book clubs that sell paper versions. The second type of book club – and what most people think of when they hear a book club mentioned – works as a readers' group.

For an informative and fun page on books and literature in general try **www.bbc.co.uk/arts/books**. Linked in with the UK daytime TV show, **www.richardandjudybookclub.co.uk** is a popular site containing reviews and recommendations and an online discussion group called The Green Room. It also has reading notes for all the titles featured in the groups. Books from its lists are available via the website at discounted prices.

Also available from the British Arts Council is **www.encom passculture.com** a site that offers book lists, author interviews, writers in residence (and a blog), advice on reading groups and much more. They cater for all ages and most literary tastes.

If you would love to belong to a book group so you can share your opinion on the books you are reading, but just don't have the time or can't get to one, try **www.bookgrouponline.com** This is an independent group that allows members to drop in read, comment, discuss as and when they want. Registration is free, and it is open 24 hours a day (useful for people like me who seem to do most of their reading at about 1 a.m.).

Tied in with the UK newspaper *The Guardian*, another useful and comprehensive book site is **http://books.guardian.co.uk/ reading/group**.

Finally in the book department, a lovely idea for exchanging books is **www.readitswapit.co.uk**. The idea is that, if you have read one book and want to read a different one, somewhere there will be someone who wants your book, and may have the one you want. So, for the price of the postage, you can swap.

Music stations

One of my favourites things to do whilst I am working is to listen to some restful music (or, if I am filing, some non-restful, motivating music), but although I have quite a few CDs in my collection that I could play on my computer, I often can't decide what to listen to. This is where online music stations come in handy.

Just like a conventional station you would get on your stereo or in your car, these stations are usually dedicated to a particular genre of music, for instance blues or jazz, 60s music etc, and can play on your computer (assuming you have a sound card and speakers, of course) while you type, surf the internet or even e-mail.

To listen to a music station (or any other radio station for that matter), you will need software such as Windows Media Player or Real Player, which can be downloaded for free from **www.real.com**.

Don't worry about media programs

You don't have to know which of these programs you will need. The computer should work it out for itself.

For instance, from Korea is **www.fallingstars.co.kr** playing pop and rock on Channel 1, and blues and jazz on Channel 2. What more can you ask for?

Jazz enthusiasts might like to try **www.jazzfm.com**, which has two options for your listening pleasure, depending how you like it. If you fancy a bit of a discussion about your favourite music or musicians, there are a number of music forums available and blogs to discuss jazz topics.

If you are feeling indecisive, or you just want to know what is out there, try **www.Shoutcast.com**. You can select your genre for music and read information about what is available, and even get a rough idea of what is playing at the moment. Simply click on the link that takes your fancy.

One of the more popular sites on the internet at the moment is **www.last.fm**, which is a combination of music station and social networking site. You type in an artist you like and they will play it and recommend similar artists. You can also see who else is listening to the same music.

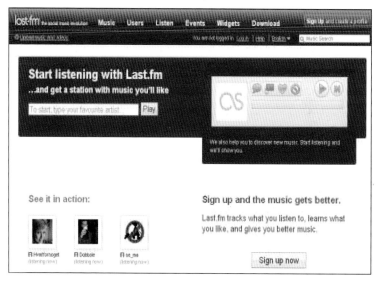

Once your music is playing, you can minimise the window and keep listening while you do other things.

Listen again

The BBC archives many of its programmes of dramas, readings and comedy for seven days after transmission before replacing them with new shows. Some factual broadcasts, e.g. *Today*, *Woman's Hour* and most science programmes are available for longer periods

One such programme is the long-running radio serial *The Archers*, where you can listen again to the individual episodes or the week's omnibus.

- From Internet Explorer, go to www.bbc.co.uk.
- Click on Radio, then select **Radio 4**.
- From the Radio 4 homepage, click **The Archers**.
- Click on **Catch up** and select the episode that you want.

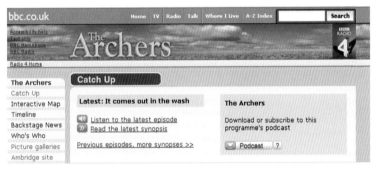

A new window will open with the Radio Player and that instantly recognisable theme tune. Due to its immense popularity, *The Archers* has its own pages, including written summaries of past episodes, quizzes and Fantasy Archers where listeners dream up scenarios for the inhabitants of Ambridge. There are also notice boards to discuss the latest goings on, picture galleries and quizzes.

Chapter 9

Meeting People

So, having looked at groups, forums and networking, it's about time that we looked at meeting people, and the possibilities of using the internet to create a social life for ourselves.

Don't be put off if you have heard scare stories about meeting people via the internet. By exercising a little common sense, and following some sensible rules, meeting people via the internet should not be any more dangerous than anywhere else. The rules for meeting people in a platonic way should not differ from those applied for meeting people in a romantic way and, if you follow them, you could have a lot of fun.

Some safety rules

- Choose a reputable website. This applies whether it be for romance or reunions. Make sure the site has a good privacy policy, and is not going to give out any of your personal details without your approval.

- Make sure your user name and details don't give away too much information about you. (Bermondsey_Barbara may be a bit of a giveaway.)

- Use a web-based separate e-mail account such as Hotmail or Yahoo, and choose an e-mail address that does not contain any personal information. Many meeting websites offer an inbox within the site, so you can check e-mail online and have no need to give out your own e-mail address.

- Get to know the person you are dealing with before you arrange a meeting. Remember: photographs can be fake, as can the description. Just because they say they are one thing does not mean they are. However, don't forget there are also many people out there just like you, so don't let the odd rogue put you off.

- Talk to each other, not just by e-mail but actually on the telephone. Again, I would suggest using a service like Skype, so you don't have to give out your actual telephone number until you are ready to do so. Hearing someone's voice is not only a great way to start a relationship, but also will give you a better idea of who this person is and whether there are any inconsistencies in their story.

Assuming you have e-mailed, talked, exchanged photographs and are sure that you are both looking forward to meeting up, this is the really important part with its own set of rules.

- Meet in a place you know your way around.

- Always meet and stay in a populated public place.

- Travel there under your own steam. Do not accept a lift from the person you are meeting.

- Tell a friend or family member who you are meeting, where you are going and when you will be back.

- Stay sober.

- Take your mobile phone.

- Your personal belongings can be stolen, your drink can be drugged. Don't leave them unattended.

If you follow these basic rules, all you have to worry about if dating is a broken heart!

Friendships old and new

There are a number of sites available now for meeting people not for dating but just for friends to get together. Some are for renewing old friendships and some are for creating new ones. One of the best known sites is Friends Reunited (**www.friends reunited.co.uk**). Originally set up to put old school friends in touch again, it now encompasses colleges and universities, work places, armed forces, clubs and even streets.

It is simple to register and if you just want to see who else has registered (and, let's be truthful, have a quick look if they have got a photo on) then there is no charge. However, if you want to send an e-mail to someone who has registered on the site, you need to buy membership, which is currently £7.50 for six months.

- From Internet Explorer, go to www.friendsreunited.co.uk.

- Click on **Register here free** to open the registration form.
- Fill in your details.

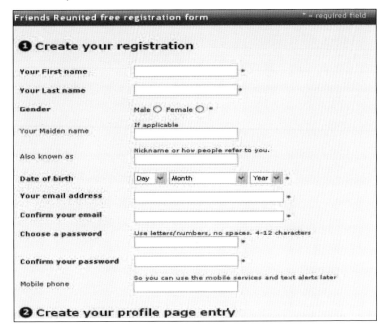

If you have married or otherwise changed your name, your school friends will not recognise this! Always put the name you would have been known by.

When you have completed your details, you can add some extra information with your profile, which tells people what country you are living in, whether you are or were married, whether you have any children and what you are doing now in your work profile.

You can also add a photo to your profile (see page 131).

Don't worry **about maintaining your privacy**

If you don't want to give all this information out, you can still register as long as you give your name and date of birth.

You also have the option of registering under the same details for Genes Reunited, the family history version of the site, Friends Reunited Chatting (for access to the site's chatrooms) and for Friends Reunited Dating (see page 136). By doing this, you only have to fill in your details once and remember one password and user name, but if you would rather not do so at this time, then leave the boxes.

- Click **Submit**.

This takes you to a page that allows you to choose where you want to register yourself: school, workplace, street, etc. You can choose one or all of these, depending on who you are looking for (or even who you hope might be looking for you).

Now you have to locate the precise organisation. If, for instance, you choose secondary school you will be asked for the name of the school and what country it was or is in.

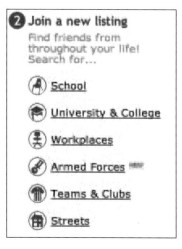

- Click on **Search** and the site will look to see whether that school in that location is registered on the website.

Remember: schools often change name, so it is possible that someone may have registered it under a different name. If you can not find the school, there are usually two reasons behind this: firstly, that you may not have remembered the name correctly (particularly easy to do when it comes to junior schools back in the aeons of time) or that the school has not been added. (You can always add it yourself and see if anyone joins in.)

The idea is normally to see who is registered from your class, so it is important that you put the correct year you left school. This does not mean that you cannot look at other years, but that if anyone from your class is looking for you and knows that they left in, for instance 1960, then that is where they would expect to find you!

Having entered your school and year of leaving you should now see a list of all the other people who were in your class. Remember, however, that if your school had a sixth form (and if you stayed to attend it) there will be people from previous classes and your classmates who did not attend sixth form who will show in the year that you *could* have left.

To find out about any of your listed classmates just click on their name. Most people give a brief history of whether they married, had children, stayed married and where they live now. If you have not paid for membership you can still let that person know you looked at their profile by sending a 'buzz' – a short message such as 'I stopped by' or 'remember me?', which will go to their inbox and appear on their profile.

If they want to contact you they can either buzz back or if they have full membership send an e-mail to your inbox on the site (not your personal e-mail) and you can look at it online. The website usually sends an e-mail to your normal e-mail address to tell you that there is a message waiting.

It is up to you at this point whether you want to pay the subscription fee and send them an answer back or to leave it as a buzz.

Adding a photograph

Many meeting sites ask you to add a photograph to your profile, but this is entirely up to you. Here's how to add a photograph if you want to.

- When you are creating your profile (see page 128), click on **My photos/videos**.

This will open a window and allow you the option of adding it either as part of a photograph album or to an individual place, assuming that you may have registered several places – for instance, secondary school, work and clubs or teams.

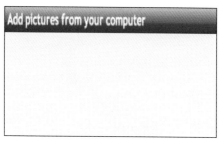

Add pictures from your computer

- Once you have chosen where the picture will appear, click on **Browse** to find on your computer the photo you wish to use. The name of the picture and its size will appear in the window Selected files. Alternatively, you may just drag and drop your photo.

- Click on **Upload**. A bar will appear showing you the progress of your file or files (depending on how big the files are, or how many there are, the amount of time taken to upload will differ).

- Click on **My Photos/Videos** and you can see the picture and add any captions or details that you would like to appear.

- When you have finished, click on **Save**.

If you decide you hate the photograph you have used, or you get a lovely new hair cut and would rather use this, then you can always delete the existing photo and replace it with the new glamorous you!

Making new friends

So we have looked at renewing old friendships, but what about making new friends? Let's start with a look at another part of Friends Reunited: **www.friendsreunitedconnections.co.uk**.

This site is very similar to the general site, but with one essential difference: chatrooms. Now, I know the media is often keen on portraying chatrooms as some sort of online den of iniquity, put there solely to facilitate sexual activity (or cybersex as it is known). Yes, there are rooms like that on the internet. However, there are also a lot of people who genuinely simply enjoy talking to other people all over the world via a chatroom.

What is a chatroom?

Depending on the site you are using, it is a space designated to an online, text-based (typed) conversation with one person or more, often on a specific subject or agenda. For instance a 'room' can be put aside for fifty-somethings to chat in, although that does not by any means exclude people of other ages joining in.

Chatrooms are open spaces, but they should have rules on what is and isn't acceptable behaviour. These could include not allowing users to use offensive language or to promote hate mail, violence and other negative issues. Also, chatrooms often do not allow advertising in their rooms or 'flooding', which is continually filling the screen with repetitive text. Typing with caps lock on is usually considered shouting and is discouraged.

Sometimes chatrooms have moderation patrols on the site, looking for disruptive or undesirable behaviour. However, you need to be aware that many chatrooms are not moderated and users may type whatever they want.

How does it work?

Firstly you have to be registered. If you signed up for this when you created your profile on Friends Reunited, you are ready to go. If not, then the procedure is much the same as any other registration, and the same safety rules should apply. Again, I would strongly recommend creating a user name that does not reflect any of your personal details.

Once you are registered take a moment to have a look around and see who is also registered.

- Click on **Search people** to discover if there is anyone of your age, or with similar interests to you.

Having chosen a room that you like the look of, you need to join it. Some rooms are moderated by setting a limit to how many people are allowed in at any given time. If you look at the one below, you will see a typical, if unpopulated, room.

The main box is set aside for people to type their messages; as they send messages they appear with their names and comments. The names of the people in the room appear on the right, and on many sites if you click on the name you can see the profile to get an idea of who you are talking to. People can join in conversations or just read the comments without joining in.

Chatrooms work very much like IM in Messenger or similar applications (see page 44). Indeed, some versions can use voice and web cams, but this appears to be more the secure way.

Many people talk to the same chatroom users day after day and build up quite a camaraderie. If you do have someone that you want to talk to away from the room, then you can invite them for a private chat. This means that any conversations you have are between you two, and cannot be seen by other people. Both parties must agree to the private chat for it to happen, and many people are quite suspicious of these, especially if they are online for friendship and have concerns that interest being shown is above and beyond this.

- When you are ready to go or want to join another chat, simply click on **Leave this room** and you are back to the main page.

Also available from Age Concern is **babyboomerbistro.org.uk** designed specifically for the over 50s and including a moderated room.

The site holds regular quizzes in the members' lounge and has discussion boards available to registered users.

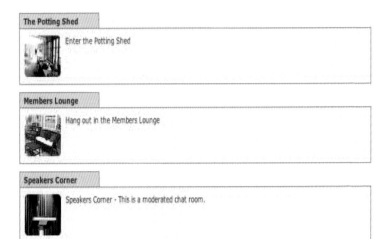

Another site aimed specifically at the over 50s is Over Fifties Friends (**www.overfiftiesfriends.co.uk**). This is a recent site set up to enable over 50s to communicate with each other and plan events. It also has a chatroom, but this is only open to members. At the time of writing, membership fees were £10 a year. The site also has job opportunities, competitions, forums and articles relevant to over 50s.

Unacceptable chat

If you happen to be in a chatroom or any online situation where someone makes you feel uneasy, or you feel that their conversation is inappropriate, you can do two things. Firstly, you can block them. This is similar to blocking a call, and means that they can no longer contact you. Secondly, if you really feel that their behaviour is wrong, you should report them to the site moderators (the people who are actually running the website), so they can look into the matter and take whatever action is appropriate.

Online dating

We've looked at friendships both old and new, and the pros and cons of looking online – but what about looking for romance online? There are hundreds of success stories out there about people who met on the internet via chatrooms or dating sites.

Online dating works in much the same way as the friendship sites. There are a vast number of online dating agencies, and you should follow the same guidelines before choosing which one to sign up with.

The first thing to do is to choose an agency, either one that caters specifically for your age group or a more general site that will encompass all ages.

Making a start

Again, Friends Reunited is a good place to start, (**www.friends reuniteddating.co.uk**), especially if you ticked the box when you initially registered. As with any meeting website, the more you say about yourself, your likes and dislikes, what you are looking for in a relationship, whether it be friendship, fun or marriage, the more chance you will have of connecting with the right person.

The first thing to do when filling in these details is to choose a user name that reflects your personality without giving too much away. I would probably suggest that if you are going to register with a number of sites that you keep the same user name and password across them all, to ensure that you can keep track of where you go.

If you are the only person using your computer then it is fairly safe on these sites to ask it to remember your user name and password (well, it will save *you* having to each time). However, if you share the computer, or are using a public computer, do not do this as you don't want to run the risk of someone getting into your account.

- From Internet Explorer go to www.friendsreunited dating.co.uk.

- Click on **Join free now** and you will be taken to the registration page.

Firstly, think about the gender and age of the person you are looking for, whether you have a specific age range in mind or you don't mind as long as that person shares your interests.

Seeking...

I am looking for *

☐ Men   you can select both
☐ Women

Aged from   * 18 [↕] to 35 [↕]

Living In   * United Kingdom [↕]

Who lives within   * 50 [↕] miles of _____ first part of my postcode e.g. KT3

For   * any type of relationship [↕]

The person you are looking for
Here's your chance to write a bit about the person you are looking for. You can be as specific or general as you like!
Please note all information is manually checked. Please **do not include contact details** or the support team will reject your notes and you will not be able to edit them.

Next, decide how far you would be willing to travel or indeed whether a long-distance relationship would suit you. You can choose to look at profiles of people within 5 to 500 miles of your postcode. Remember, however, that if you live in a rural area or a small village, you may find it difficult to meet anyone that local.

To save any confusion at a future date, it is best to be clear about what sort of relationship you are looking for. You can choose between friendship, romance, marriage and a few in between. If you know that you are very unlikely to want anything too committed, you might want to choose romance (though obviously there is nothing to say you can't change your mind at a later date, if the right offer comes along!).

So, on to you. Filling in details about yourself can be quite a painstaking process, so perhaps it would be an idea to write down what you want to say before you get on the computer. You would hope that the people you are contacting have been honest about themselves, so try to do the same. If *you* can knock 10 years off your age, then so can everyone else.

• When you have completed the boxes, click on **Next**.

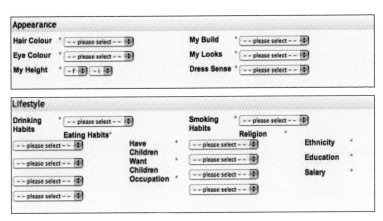

To save on typing, all you need to do is click on the drop-down boxes and select whatever fits your profile best. When you have finished describing yourself, you need to let people know what your personality is like. Click in whichever boxes are most accurate.

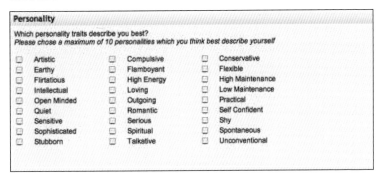

The last questions are on your favourite things, e.g., a liking for the same music or films makes a good conversational opener, so try to make sure you really add what you like. If you have never read *War and Peace*, don't put it on, because you could end up with a very disappointed Russian scholar.

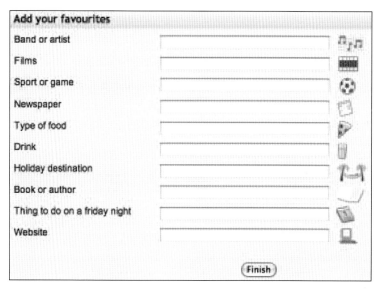

- Click **Finish**.

You will be sent a validation code to your normal e-mail address. This is to ensure that it genuinely is you filling in these details, and not possibly some misguided friend who thinks you need a date!

Follow the instructions in your e-mail, and you will return to the site and be given the opportunity to put in a photograph. This will work on most sites exactly the same way as the previous instructions I gave on page 131. Again, it is up to you whether you want to do this. A lot of people only search for profiles that have a photograph with them, so you might miss out if you don't.

- If you don't want to add a photo, or want to do it at a later date, then click on **Skip**.

Don't worry about your profile

If you don't like your profile or photo, you can go back and change it at any time.

Other dating sites

Other popular websites for dating are:

- **www.datingdirect.com:** calls itself the UK's largest dating service.

- **www.match.com:** guarantees to find you someone special within six months.

- **www.outeverywhere.com:** site specifically for anyone looking for a same sex relationship (although most sites include this) that offers a 28-day trial with membership fee.

- **www.saga.co.uk/connections:** if you would really prefer to look only within the over 50s age group.

Have fun!

Chapter 10

Employment

If you have just retired or decided to go part time, you might be finding that the days are very long and you miss the companionship of working life. Or perhaps your children have left home to go their own ways, leaving you with rather more time on your hands than you expected.

Now, I'm not suggesting that you start working again; well, not strictly speaking. But even if you don't actually want to get a job, most of us have picked up some skills along the way that we can use, potentially for other people's benefit.

Volunteering

Especially if you have retired, one of the greatest commodities you may have on your hands is time. If you do not need to work or even if you work part time, there are many organisations in desperate need of helpers. You would be surprised how often the skills that you have developed over the years that you don't bother to count as useful could be of massive benefit to someone else. Registered charity YouthNet is a non-profit-making organisation that can help you find out whether there is anything in your area you could do. There is no charge to look opportunities up on this site.

- From Internet Explorer, go to www.do-it.org.uk.

- Fill in your interest, activity and town or postcode, then click on **Find it**.

- You can extend your options by clicking on **Advanced search**.

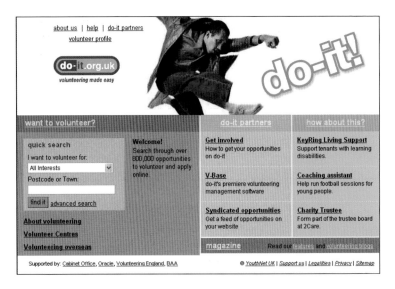

The advanced search is useful if, for instance, you only have certain days or parts of the day that you can give to volunteering, e.g. every Tuesday afternoon. You can look under particular interests such as elderly, youth, animals or museums. You can also stipulate how far from your own postcode you are willing to travel.

Other places to volunteer

- **Volunteering England (www.volunteering.org.uk):** this is an organisation that can not only show you what is available in your area, but can also advise you on what type of volunteering might suit you. That could include helping on campaigns, working on conservation and environmental projects, or running a shop or stall for fund raising.

- **Retired and Senior Volunteer Programme (RSVP) (www.csv.org.uk/Volunteer/Senior+Volunteers/Senior+ Volunteers.htm):** a scheme run by CVS, an organisation that has definitely realised the potential of older volunteers. RSVP was founded in 1988 and aims to offer an easy way to get involved in the local community. It has over 8,500 volunteers throughout the UK.

- **RNIB Talking Book Service (www.rnib.org.uk):** a postal lending service of audio books delivered to over 40,000 blind and partially sighted people in the UK. Volunteers visit recipients in their homes to help set up equipment and sort out any problems with using the audio books.

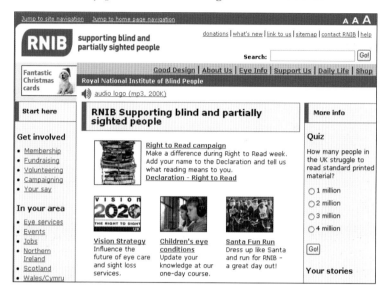

- **VSO (www.vso.org.uk):** one of the best known organisations offering the opportunity to volunteer for work abroad, this charity has been in existence since 1958. It needs volunteers between 18 and 75 years old who must have a formal qualification and some work experience. Regular postings are for two years and volunteers are provided with accommodation and a local level allowance as well as airfares and insurance.

Many other charities are looking for volunteers, not just to help out with shops and sales, but also to help people go about their daily lives. Volunteering is not only a good way to do your bit for your local community, but it is also a great way to meet people and make new friends.

Work

You may have retired or taken early retirement, been made redundant or decided that now was the time to go back to work. Whatever your reasons and whether you are looking for a full or part-time job, there are myriad websites dedicated solely to looking for work. There are also sites aimed specifically at older people.

If the reason you are now looking for a job is that you have finally had enough of commuting, or you have moved to your dream home but need to work, the chances are you will want to look for work locally. Obviously this is not going to be available for everyone, but there are sites that will tailor make your searches to within a certain radius of your postcode (also very helpful if you have to rely on public transport).

Registering with a job search site

One of the main things on all employment sites is the online CV; if you have not written a CV (or not for a long time) many sites have advice and step-by-step guides on how to make the most of your skills. As with many of the online entries we have made throughout this book, it is always a good idea to take a moment to sit down and think about what you want to say about yourself, to try and remember what dates are relevant in your working history and to ensure that you give a clear and concise account of why you are the best person for the job.

There are a number of sites that are specifically for jobs that are local, such as **www.fish4.co.uk/iad/jobs**. Your local newspaper is also very likely to have a website where jobs that have been advertised in the paper will appear. Try searching for your local paper using Google. Some local council websites also show jobs within the borough or county, so it may be worth checking these, too.

Monster

One of the more popular websites for jobs is Monster (created by the same person who brought you Eons – see page 103) and it has a specific search for local vacancies (**www.monster. co.uk/local**). This page has direct links to the major UK cities and you just click on your nearest.

- However, if none of this is close enough, click on **Find jobs**. A window will open that allows you to enter your postcode and the distance in miles that you would be willing to travel.

- Next choose what industry you would like to work in, for instance Retail or Performing & Fine Arts, and the type of work such as Administrative/Clerical or Training/ Instruction.

- Select whether you are looking for permanent or temporary work, full or part time and whether you would consider working at home.

If there is a very specific word that you know will be included in any job titles or description that would interest you, enter it as a keyword. Be warned, however, that unless this is essential, including keywords can limit the amount of returns in any search, so do not put one in if you are just trying to get a general feel of what is available in your range.

- Specify how you would like to be told about jobs that match your criteria.

Think about whether you would like to be told each time a potentially suitable job comes up. Monster offers a Job Search Agent, as do many other job sites, that will e-mail you lists of jobs and details of the jobs on a regular basis. You can choose whether to have them daily, weekly or monthly. If you would rather not have them, then do not tick the box. Remember that you will have to check your e-mail if you want to keep up with the available jobs.

You can also choose how you want jobs to appear: either in date order or in relevance to your search criteria. Your last choice on this site is how much detail you want to see at first glance – whether you want a brief summary of what each job is or whether you want everything.

Don't worry **about choices**

If you make the wrong choice, you can always go back and change things.

Government help

If you are worried about looking for work that is geared towards your age group in particular, or that you might miss out on work because of your age, try **www.jobcentreplus.gov.uk**. This is a government website and is part of the Job Centre.

This site also deals with advice and benefits, as well as with the scheme New Deal 50 Plus. If you are eligible for this, you will be offered a personal adviser to help you choose what sort of work would be suitable for your skills. You will also receive help in looking for and applying for jobs, and any relevant training opportunities. There is also advice on securing voluntary work that may help with getting the job you want.

If you find work through this scheme, you can also apply for an in-work training grant of up to £1,500 to improve your skills and help you progress or to get a better job. Jobcentre Plus can also help with benefits and tax credits.

Also from the government, **www.agepositive.gov.uk/ jobseeking** is a site that offers both links and advice.

Finally, **www.skilledpeople.com** is aimed at the over 50s and is a free-to-register website that offers job searching facilities and volunteering opportunities for people with experience.

Starting your own business

If you have reached the stage in your life where you feel that you have had enough of working for other people, and that being your own boss sounds more and more attractive, pay a visit to Business Link (**www.businesslink.gov.uk**). It offers advice on everything from starting up, how to decide whether the business you think would suit you really would, to how to create a business plan and avoid the common mistakes when starting up. It also offers advice on finance, taxes, health and safety, IT and e-commerce, marketing and how to try to ensure your business grows.

Another website that is dedicated to helping the over 50s to set up business is Prime Initiative (the Prince's Initiative for Mature Enterprise) (**www.primeinitiative.org.uk** or in Wales **www.prime-cymru.co.uk**). This is a registered charity linked to Age Concern England, founded by HRH The Prince of Wales, PRIME's President, and a member of the Prince's Charities Group. It offers free information and help, workshops and business networking events. It can also refer you to properly accredited advisers for free business advice, and can provide help and advice on starting a social enterprise.

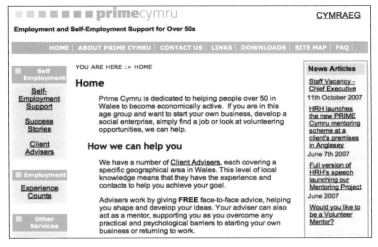

I would also recommend looking at Later Life (**www.later life.com**) a general website for the over 50s, but with a section on starting your own business, that has a number of useful links to help and advice.

Working from home

There are many opportunities available for working from home. Some appear to be more lucrative than they actually are, while others can probably net you a decent income if you are willing to put the work in. Some employers are genuine and some are scammers. Like everywhere, the unwary can be taken advantage of on the internet.

If a company is asking for money up front before it will even tell you what the product is going to be, then it very unlikely to be above board. Many companies that appear to be offering jobs are actually trying to sell you information on how they say you 'could' make money working from home.

Many high-street employment agencies have work from home jobs, and it would be worth your while to register with some locally, if this is what you have decided will suit you. If you are looking for something a little more ad hoc, then you should follow some basic rules to ensure that you earn money rather than end up spending it!

Now you know how to use the internet and, more importantly, how to do a search, use these skills to research any company that offers you work. Find out whether they exist, find out if anyone has put something on the internet about them – there are websites set up for complaints. Try **www.grumbletext.co.uk** or **www.moneysavingexpert.com**, either of which may have comments from other people who have had dealings with the companies in question.

If you are looking at earning some money for treats rather than to pay bills, here are some of the opportunities available:

Mystery shopping

For the purposes of market research, customer satisfaction and improvement in staff performance, many organisations employ companies to spot check the way they operate. A mystery shopper can be in person, online or on the telephone. Operating to a prearranged scenario, it would be your role to find out how much staff know about products, or how quickly you get served or even just how polite and helpful staff are.

For further information, try **www.retaileyes.co.uk** or **www.tns-global.com**.

Online surveys

There are a number of these companies on the internet and it is easy to get involved. Firstly you need to register, which is free. Fill in as many details about you as you can. This helps make sure that they don't send you survey offers on subjects you couldn't possibly know about.

Once you are registered, you will be sent an e-mail offering you the chance to take part in whatever surveys they believe you may have an opinion on, whether this be lifestyle, detergents or hotels. All you have to do is study the questions, and answer them honestly as they relate to you. Surveys can take five minutes or half an hour, depending on the subject matter.

Don't worry **if you don't meet the criteria**

Often you will be sent a survey that when you sign in you will find that you do not meet their criteria. This is irritating, but another, more appropriate one should follow soon.

Although you will not make your fortune from these, they are a handy way to practise your computer skills, keep your brain sharp and make a bit of money whilst clicking or typing brief answers. The rewards vary between companies and depend on the survey and the length of time they believe it will take to complete. Some companies pay a cash amount that goes into an account held online for you and you can redeem it after it reaches a certain level. Others pay in vouchers for big brand stores, and some enter you into a prize draw. Each survey will stipulate how much it is worth before you start it, whether it is 27p, £1.50 or points.

For surveys for cash payments go to **www.ciao.co.uk** or **www.yougov.com**. In the latter, your account is credited up to £50 then you will receive payment, or entry into a prize draw depending on the survey.

YouGov Awards

The many successes of YouGov, securing its position at the leading edge of the market research industry, have been rewarded by a number of prestigious awards

For payment in vouchers, go to **http://gb.lightspeedpanel.com** or **www.valuedopinions.co.uk**, where points are available as vouchers after you have reached £10.

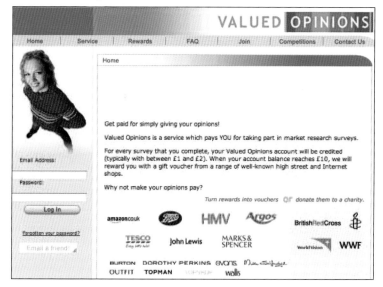

For payment in Nectar points, go to **www.mytns.com**.

Another option is **www.mutualpoints.com**, where you get points for clicking on links to given websites and more points for then buying on these sites. Remember, this is only a bargain if you had intended buying the goods in the first place; if you find yourself buying to get points you are rather defeating the purpose! This site also offers points for signing up for e-mail offers, and then clicking on the offers to go to the website. This would mean an increase in the amount of spam coming in to your inbox but, as with all of these offers, it could earn you a little money everyday to put aside for something.

I cannot emphasise enough that none of the above web schemes will make enough money to live on (or if so I am doing something wrong!), but a steady trickle of surveys mounts up faster than you would imagine and if you are signed up for a few different ones you can accumulate a few pounds.

Buying and selling on eBay

On the subject of making your computer work for you there are a few other options you may wish to consider.

Combining your hobby with your internet skills, you could look into selling duplicate or surplus items on an auction site such as eBay. If you know your subject, and have time to go and find replacement stock, you could actually start trading on there (although there are different types of account, depending on how much you are buying and selling through the site). There are many advantages to using an auction site to sell goods if you know your subject: not having to pay rent and commercial taxes for premises would certainly count quite highly on my list.

There is very little that you cannot buy on eBay: from books to houses and there are various ways that it works.

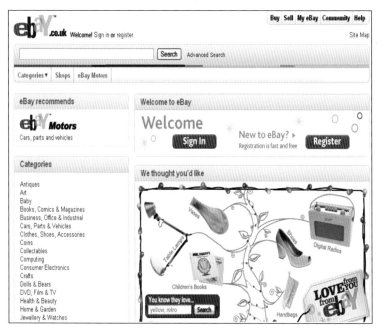

Before you start using eBay, I would recommend having a good look around the website, and learn how the site works. The first time you buy something here, go for something quite small and inexpensive, rather than an item that is going to cost you a lot if it is either wrong or not quite what you expected.

I have bought many things from eBay over the years, from books and DVDs to watches and even laptop computers, all of which have been good value and what I wanted. There are a number of safeguards in place on the site to try and stop people from getting duped, but the best advice I can give is to always know the value of the item you are bidding on, as it is easy to get carried away.

Selling on eBay

I would suggest that you thoroughly read the seller's tutorial on the eBay website, but here are the salient points:

- From Internet Explorer, go to www.eBay.co.uk. (This is an international site, so you need the 'uk'.)

- Create a seller's account.

Register with eBay Help ?

Register today to bid, buy or sell on eBay.

Already registered or want to make changes to your account? Sign in.
Want to open an account for your business?

Business sellers should register with a business account. Learn more about business registration.

Tell us about yourself - All fields are required

[i] Your privacy is important to us. eBay does not rent or sell your personal information to third parties without your consent. To learn more, read our privacy policy. Your address will be used for posting your purchase or receiving payment from buyers.

First name

Last name

Street address

Already registered?

Sign in now or enter your confirmation code to activate your account.

- Resend my confirmation code
- Resend my password
- Resend my user ID

This will involve you giving all your details exactly as you would on any other registration, but this time they will also require a credit or debit card and your bank details for verification purposes.

There are fees for placing an item on eBay, broken down into an insertion fee, which is the amount you pay depending on the value of the goods you are selling, and a final value fee, which reflects the price you actually get. Current fees are available on the site.

Insertion Fees		Final Value Fees	
Starting or Reserve Price	**Insertion Fee**	**Closing Price**	**Final Value Fee**
£0.01 - £0.99	**£0.15**	Item not sold	No Fee
£1.00 - £4.99	**£0.20**	£0.01 - £29.99	**5.25%** for the amount of the high bid (at the listing close for auction-style listings) up to £29.99
£5.00 - £14.99	**£0.35**		
£15.00 - £29.99	**£0.75**	£30.00 - £599.99	**5.25%** of the initial £29.99 (£1.57), plus **3.25%** of the remaining closing value balance
£30.00 - £99.99	**£1.50**		
£100.00 or more	**£2.00**	Over £600.00	**5.25%** of the initial £29.99 (£1.57), plus **3.25%** of the initial £30.00 - £599.99 (£18.53), plus **1.75%** of the remaining closing value balance
for multiple item listings in £100.00 or more tier	**£3.00**		

- Look at the listings already on the site.

Are the any items similar to the one you want to sell? Check what price they are listed at, what condition they are listed as and any other details that will affect your sale.

- Decide what type of listing you want.

This could be auction, fixed price or buy it now (though you need to have sold several items previously to qualify for this). Bear in mind if you are selling in an auction and you do not set a reserve, then you could end up selling for 1p if that is what you are offered. I have bought items in the past where the postage has cost more than the goods.

- Describe the item.

As well as a basic description of the item you are selling, you need to state whether it is new or used, what condition it is in and any extra hooks that you think will make it attractive to buyers. If possible, include a photograph, because buyers like to see what they are getting.

- Include the cost for postage and packing.

Some goods such as cars or bikes cannot be posted, or you might be unwilling to attempt to post goods that are, for instance, very fragile. In these cases, you should stipulate 'buyer collects'. If your item can be posted then you should be able to tell buyers how much this will cost. Don't forget to factor into these costs the price of wrapping and envelopes as well as postage. If you are willing to send abroad you should put 'worldwide' on your listing, and also advise costs for Europe, USA, etc.

- Specify how you would like payment.

Many buyers prefer to make payment using PayPal. This is eBay's own automatic electronic payment system, and is safe, carries some insurance and is very quick. There are no fees for buyers but sellers are charged. However, if this is the difference between getting sales or not then I would suggest that you include it as a factor in your calculations of a reserve price. If you do not manage to sell your item, eBay will let you re-list it for free. You can also opt to receive payment by credit card or cheque. Always ensure that you have payment cleared before releasing the item.

Other sources of information

- **ByteStart (www.bytestart.co.uk):** has guides on how to start a business.

- **Work From Home Guide (www.workfromhomeguide.net):** a comprehensive list of potential pitfalls, plus some very sensible advice on the dos and don'ts of working from home. Although the site is American and therefore quite a few of the laws mentioned here will not apply, the general concept on what is right or wrong remains the same, and I really like the no-nonsense approach of its creator.

- **Home Business Ideas (www.experienced-people.co.uk/ 5002-home-based-business-ideas):** a UK site with some good ideas about home working.

Chapter 11
Learning

There is a saying that you are never too old to learn. However, there does not appear to be a saying that tells you exactly when you are going to have the time to do so! Many people have promised themselves that they would get that degree, or do that course on whatever or even get the qualifications they could have left school with had they not discovered girls/boys/music/earning money, and so on.

One of the other reasons for studying is work. Many older people feel left out of job opportunities due to a lack of knowledge of new technologies. Some people just fancy a better or different job as they become older and then need to retrain or get a formal qualification in order to follow their chosen career path.

If you have to go to work or have other commitments, finding time to travel to a course in a college or similar, do the course and travel back – not to mention the time you need to put in on homework or coursework – can make it a rather daunting prospect.

However, as I am sure you will have guessed, I am about to tell you how to do a course from the comfort of your own home using the internet. I will also tell you how to find courses that you can go to in your area, and a few other examples of less formal learning that may broaden your horizons.

Online learning

Online learning is also often known as e-learning or distance learning and is used to refer to learning that takes place using the internet for some or all of the time.

There are advantages and disadvantages to learning on the internet. On the plus side you can suit your own timetable and if you miss a slot you don't have to wait a week before the next class. The down side is that you don't get to socialise with your classmates and you have to be really self-disciplined and ensure you go online regularly.

Many people believe that the only courses on the internet are about the internet! This is not true. Although there are a number of excellent courses available to improve your computer skills, there are also thousands of other courses on most subjects that you can name.

Learning with the BBC

Take some time to explore the BBC site, which covers everything from languages to science.

• From Internet Explorer, go to www.bbc.co.uk/learning.

As you will see, there are quick links to a wide range of subjects, including computer skills.

- If you are not sure what section you want or you have a specific course in mind, click on **Course search**.

This links to other courses available both as taught courses (in a classroom setting) or self study. Let's practise with a look at language courses.

- Click on **Languages**.

Always fancied a trip to Provence? Let's select French.

- Click on **French**, then choose the level you want.

- Click on **Gauge your knowledge** if you are not sure which course will suit your knowledge.

You might be surprised how much you remember – I know I was. If you already speak some French, or you want just enough to get by then there are options for this. If you want a broader vocabulary, more than, say, just being able to order a drink or say please and thank you appropriately, then sign up for intermediate classes. If your French is quite good, but not good enough to cover working in France or a longer stay, click on **Other resources** and embark on **The French Experience**.

- Assuming you are going to start from scratch, click on **French Steps**.

This will enable you to create a membership. There is no charge for these courses and if you sign up as a member you can keep track of your progress as you go along to remind you which units you have done and how you did with them.

French Steps is made up of 24 short steps or units: Taking a taxi, Asking for directions, organised into six sections: Short break in Paris, Food and drink, etc. devised to be used in short sessions, so this course should suit even the most demanding of schedules.

The really good thing about courses like these is that you can listen (and listen again as many times as you want or need) to the correct way to pronounce and phrase sentences, not like the days of learning purely from a book and a slightly frazzled French teacher!

Also on the page is a 'quick fix' printable list of keywords or expressions you might find useful if you were about to go on holiday to France but didn't speak the language.

Don't worry about looking at children's sites

Don't be ashamed! The BBC Bitesize pages aimed at GCSE revision are a good resource and more fun than the grown-up version!

Other BBC resources

Many of the BBC courses also tie in with programmes on the BBC Two Learning Zone on during the night (no, I am not suggesting staying up all night, but that you can record programmes to work on at your leisure). For instance, between 2 and 6 a.m. there will be a number of video presentations covering all topics from getting around, shopping, work and even talking to a chemist. There are also pages aimed at helping you improve your ability to learn languages with some tips on making the course work best for you.

If you have no interest in languages (or speak so many that you don't need any more), try Gardening that ties in with advice from the TV programme *Gardeners' World*.

If you like classical music but don't really know much about it, look at A Quick Guide to Classical, where you will find a list covering the last 900 years broken down into timescales and composers. Clicking on the name of a composer will give you information on when and where they lived, the major works attributed to them and a brief sound clip to give you an idea of what they sound like. If you spend a lot of time hearing pieces of music and wondering who and what, this could be the course for you.

Before we leave the BBC website to look at some of the other sites available, I must first recommend the Webwise course, an essential for newcomers to get sensible answers to puzzling computer questions. The site is presided over by Bruce who is a spider, so if in doubt, **Ask Bruce**.

Learndirect

One of the well-known online learning providers that is found at the end of many of the links on the BBC site is Learndirect (**www.learndirect.co.uk**). Launched in 2000, more than two million learners have enrolled on almost 4.5 million of its courses, which cover a wide range of topics at various levels, including management, IT and languages, with more than three-quarters of the courses available online.

Learndirect also offers a free advice service providing information and guidance to help adults make decisions on learning and work opportunities. It also has an enhanced guidance service offering personalised careers direction for people who are returning to work, who have been made redundant or are facing redundancy.

If you don't want to study on your own at home or if your computer or internet access is insufficient for any long time use, you can attend a Learndirect centre (there are over 800 in the UK at the time of writing) where you can have access to a computer and the internet, and ask a tutor to help you if you get stuck.

If you have any doubt about your skills and what you want or need to learn or even if you know your subject but want to brush up on it in order to gain a formal qualification, Learndirect offers a skills and interests assessment – where I was glad to discover that based on the answers I gave that I am doing the right job!

There is a fee for courses (with the exception of adult literacy and numeracy courses), but these differ for each course and are dependant on the circumstances of the applicant. There are often government incentives that will help with fees for further education, particularly if they are work related.

Working very closely with Learndirect are the UK Online centres (www.ufi.com/ukol). The aim of the these is to provide computer and internet access to anyone who wants it, so if you do not have your own computer or cannot get to a Learndirect centre, it is worth checking to see whether there is one of these centres nearby.

Open University

Very few people have not heard of the Open University (**www.open.ac.uk**), one of the oldest distance learning organisations around today. I am sure, however, that many people do not realise quite how many courses at all different levels it offers.

I must admit to having thought it was primarily for degrees and higher level academic qualifications (which it continues to offer), but it also offers stand-alone certificates and diplomas, – all of which can count towards any other degrees you may decide to take – and foundation degrees.

At present the OU offers over 580 courses in 13 main categories: business and management; education and teacher training; environment; health and social care/health studies; humanities: arts, languages, history; information technology and computing; law and criminology; mathematics and statistics; psychology, philosophy, politics, economics; science; social sciences; technology, engineering and manufacturing; and continuing professional development.

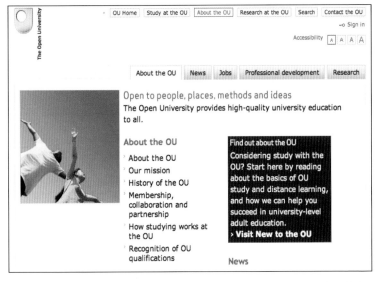

Course fees differ enormously depending on the length of the course, and the qualification you are aiming at. As a rough example, a nine-month course would cost somewhere in the region of £400 and a BSc (Honours) degree could cost about £4,000, but this can be spread over several years, depending on how quickly you study. There is financial support available for some people so I would recommend checking to see whether you are eligible for either help with your fees or money towards your computer.

If you are working and the qualification would help in your job, you might find that your employer will sponsor you for some of the fees. The excellent thing is that everyone recognises the name and the OU continues to have a good reputation.

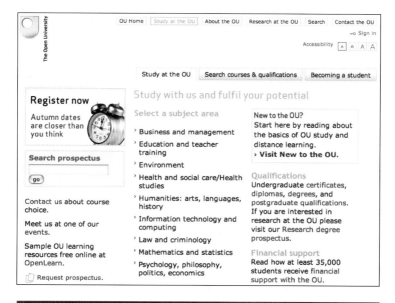

Learning IT

There are many sites that can help you to learn more about IT and gain a qualification. Bear in mind, though, that there is no point in signing up for long, complicated courses unless you are willing to put in the time and effort. If you only need to learn the basics, try to start with a free beginner's course and see if you get on with the style of learning on offer.

- **Computeach (www.computeach.co.uk):** one of the longer running companies that can help you to learn more about IT and gain a qualification. There are fees involved and some of the courses take several years to complete. The courses are run with books, interactive CDs or DVDs and the internet or sometimes via one of the centres in London or the West Midlands.

As with many of the online training companies, it operates an online forum for students to share experiences or discuss the course. As with any commercial company that offers training, check that it can supply the level of support you need before you commit any sums of money.

- **Alison (www.alison.com):** a relatively new site that is free to individual learners and one of the sites that I have been looking at with great interest. It covers ECDL (European Computer Driving Licence), IT literacy and touch-typing and according to its website will be offering further courses in the future. Course pages do have advertising on them (which is how the site remains free), but I did not find that intrusive.

- **The Virtual University (http://vu.org):** an internet community that proudly boasts: 'Since 1995, more than two million learners from 128 countries have attended classes at our global village campus!' It charges a flat fee of $20 a term and you can take up to four classes concurrently. When you register it creates a virtual desk for you and all your work goes on to it. Lessons are posted once a week. Bear in mind this is an American site and works on Pacific Time. Most lessons are posted on a Sunday night, but you would need to check individual classes.

It recommends spending three to four hours a week on homework, reading and general study and discussion per topic. Each classroom has a discussion board where you can swap ideas with other people taking the same classes (remember to take the same safety precautions I have been drumming into you all the way through this book).

Every course has a final exam (you knew there would be a catch) that consists of randomly selected multiple-choice questions. Each exam has grades depending on how many questions you get right and these make up an 'eTranscript', which is posted on to your account at VU. A grade of 70 points or more is considered a pass.

According to the website a pass entitles you to continuing education units (CEU), which may be of use in any further academic endeavours in the future, but this might not be applicable beyond the USA. However, if you are just looking to learn new things for the sheer pleasure this looks like one of the more interesting and friendly sites I have seen for a while.

- **Techademic (www.techademic.com)**: offers computer course holidays exclusively for the over 50s.

- **Digital Unite (www.digitalunite.net):** a company with trainers based around the country for those of you who prefer to learn how to use your computer in the comfort of your own home and be taught by someone of your own age.

- **UCanDoIT (www.ucandoit.org.uk):** a London-based charity teaches registered disabled people internet skills in their own home for a small fee (based on income). At present it does not have tutors in many places outside London, but this may change so check the website.

Learning locally

For many people the idea of doing all your learning, or the majority of it, in front of a computer on your own seems a little daunting and takes a lot of self-discipline. In this case a local class would seem the best answer.

For a comprehensive list of available resources for learning at 50+ go to **www.direct.gov.uk/en/Over50s/Learning/index.htm**. This site, run by the Central Office of Information, not only gives advice on studying and links to finding courses in your area, but can also help with information on funding, benefits and work-based learning.

Your local council may have information on classes in your area, usually classified under something like Lifelong Learning.

> 'More older people are also choosing to participate in education and learn new skills including the use of computers and internet. In 2002, 51% of those aged 60 to 69 in England and Wales engaged in some form of learning as opposed to 47% in 1997.' Source: *English Longitudinal Study of Ageing 2002*, University College London, 2005

Also available for women is the Townswomen's Guild, an organisation that arose from the women's suffrage movement and continues going strong to this day. Boasting 40,000 members and 1,100 branches, it is a professional organisation whose aim is to influence and educate on a broad range of subjects.

University of the Third Age

If none of the websites has courses that suit your purposes or are more academically based than you wanted, I would suggest that the place for you might be the University of the Third Age, popularly known as U3A (**www.u3a.org.uk**).

This organisation is made up of local branches that are defined as: 'self-help, self-managed lifelong learning co-operatives for older people no longer in full time work, providing opportunities for their members to share learning experiences in a wide range of interest groups and to pursue learning not for qualifications, but for fun.'

With over 600 branches and almost 200,000 members there is a distinct possibility that there will be a branch near you. Search the website to find your nearest group either by address or postcode. Membership is inexpensive and events and classes differ from branch to branch. If you live in an area with more than one branch check with each to see what they have planned for the future.

Courses are led by branch members who are willing to share their knowledge on a wide variety of topics and are often held in peoples' homes. Courses run weekly, fortnightly or monthly depending on the course leader and are usually kept to relatively small groups.

Many branches also organise trips or visits to interesting places such as National Trust properties. There are also some online courses available for U3A members ranging from art history, creative writing to digital imaging.

Educational media

There are many programs available covering education, reference (dictionaries and encyclopaedias), languages, hobbies and even home improvement. The difference between an online learning process and this software is that once you have bought it, you can load it on to your computer and have access for as long as you want.

To get an idea of the vast range of software available, look at the range offered by Amazon (**www.amazon.co.uk**), one of the largest online retailers. When I looked at their language section I got over 3,000 results – so perhaps I should have chosen a language first!

Also available are language translation programs that will help with common words in a variety of languages (English to French for instance and vice versa). I found these extremely useful when I was working on some genealogy and came across a site that was beyond my very basic French.

- To find software that suits what you want to learn, in the search box of your search engine, type, for instance, genealogy +software.

Remember also that many of the programs already on your computer have tutorials with them. Always look in the Help menu.

DVD drive

Using educational media is usually learning material on either CD-ROM or DVD. Many older computers do not have DVD drives and you should check this before ordering material. To find out what type of drive your computer has follow these steps:

- Double-click on **My Computer**, which should be on your desktop.

- If you are using Windows XP you can also access this by clicking **Start** in the bottom left-hand corner of your screen and then clicking on **My Computer**.

A window will open and a list of various drives you have will appear, identified usually as A, C and D. The D drive is most often your CD or DVD drive and it will be labelled as such. If you have a fairly new computer or laptop then it is most probable that your drive will be DVD.

So there you have it. If you want to learn something new, you might have thought it was difficult to know where to start, but now you certainly have no excuses!

Wiki it!

As an informal learning (non academic) tool try a wiki, that is, a collaborative website. There are many wikis on the web, the best know being Wikipedia, which defines itself as 'a multilingual, web-based, free content encyclopaedia project. Wikipedia is written collaboratively by volunteers from all around the world. With rare exceptions, its articles can be edited by anyone with access to the internet, simply by clicking the edit this page link. Since its creation in 2001, Wikipedia has grown rapidly into one of the largest reference Web sites.'

What that means, put simply, is that if you know something about something you can add it to this massive online encyclopaedia and share your knowledge with the world. Not only is it a very useful and sometimes fascinating tool for looking things up, but also if you scroll to the bottom of its homepage you will find Wikibooks, which are free textbooks and manuals on all sorts of subjects.

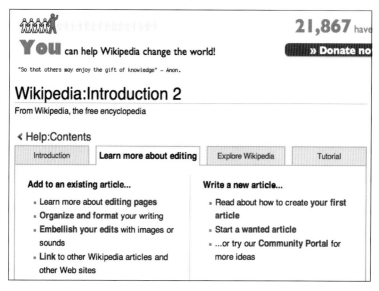

Wikipedia has different sites around the world. The main site is **www.wikipedia.org**; the English language one is at **www.en.wikipedia.org**.

Chapter 12
Conclusion

I hope that you have enjoyed going through this book and that it has helped lead you to some interesting sites.

If you have had the chance to meet old friends or make new ones, learn a new skill, got a new job, volunteered for a project that helped someone somewhere then my work is done.

There is always something new to learn, be it on or via a computer and I hope this experience has given you a taste for what can be accomplished.

Maybe you would like to share your computer skills with other people or write a blog telling the world how you found love on the web after reading this book. Perhaps you will finally take a degree or learn all about digital photography, so you can take pictures of your world trip (booked via the internet obviously!).

If you decided to start your business using the internet you may be ready to look at getting your own website. Why not learn to do it yourself? You already know that it's not as hard to do these things as you once may have imagined.

Index